HIRSCHFELD'S SONDHEIM

a poster book

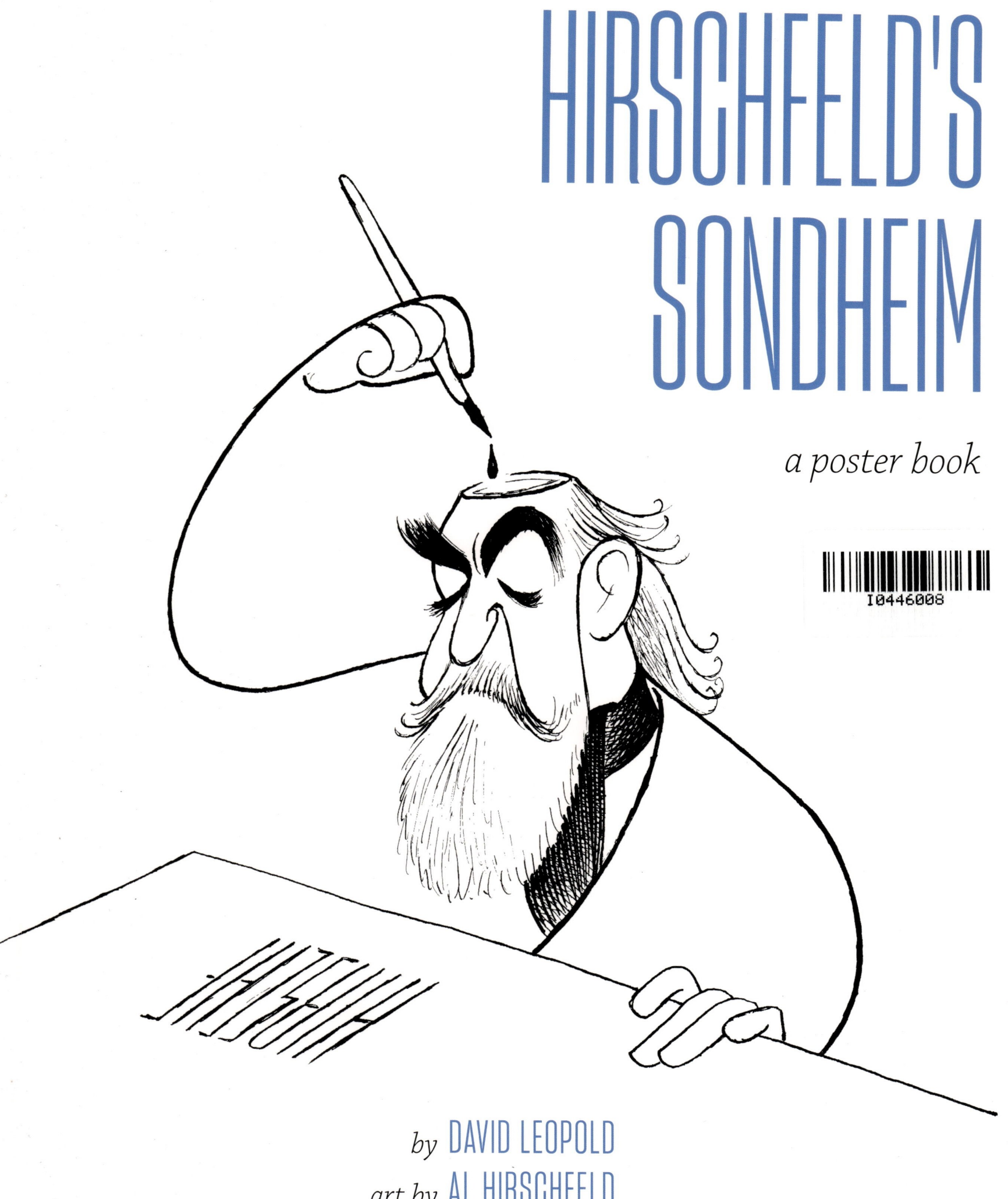

by **DAVID LEOPOLD**
art by **AL HIRSCHFELD**

introduction by **Bernadette Peters**
foreword by **Ben Brantley**

ABRAMS COMICARTS, NEW YORK

HIRSCHFELD and SONDHEIM:

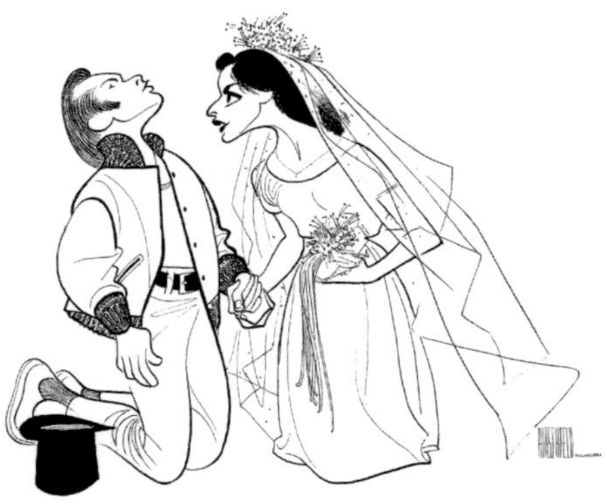

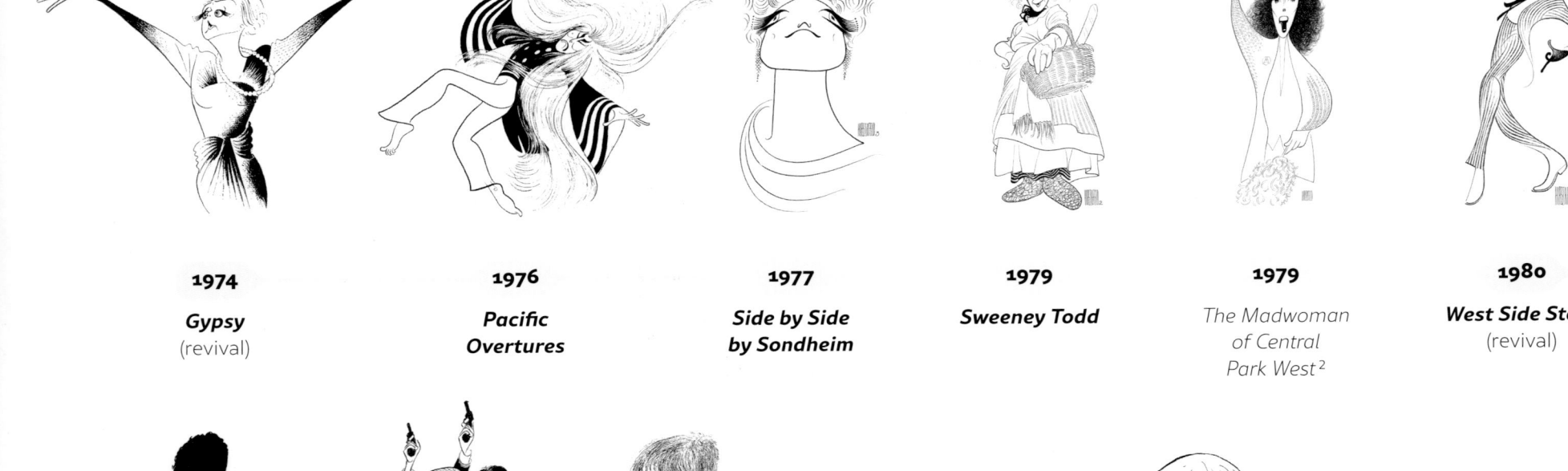

1957

West Side Story

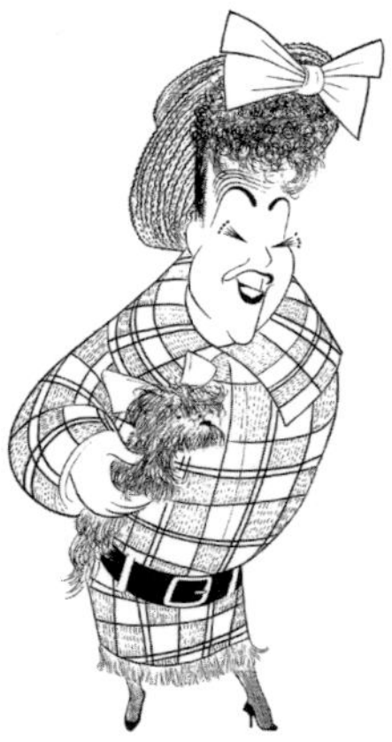

1959

Gypsy

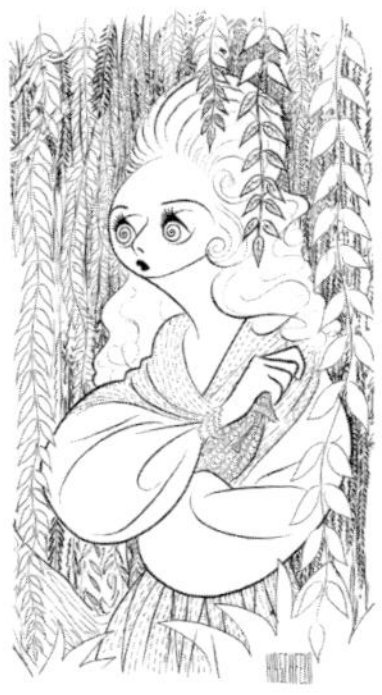

1960

*Invitation
to a March* [1]

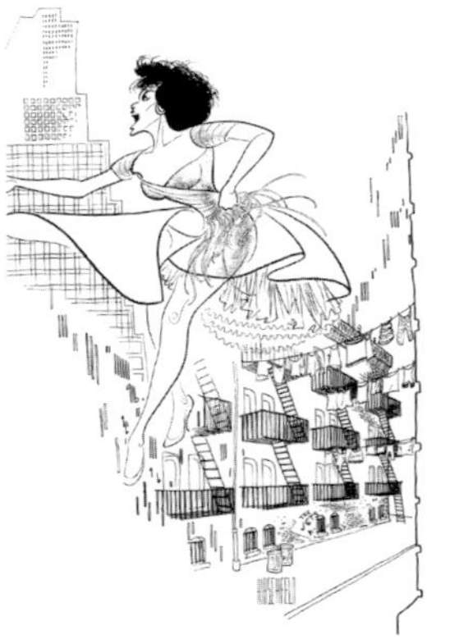

1961

West Side Story
(film)

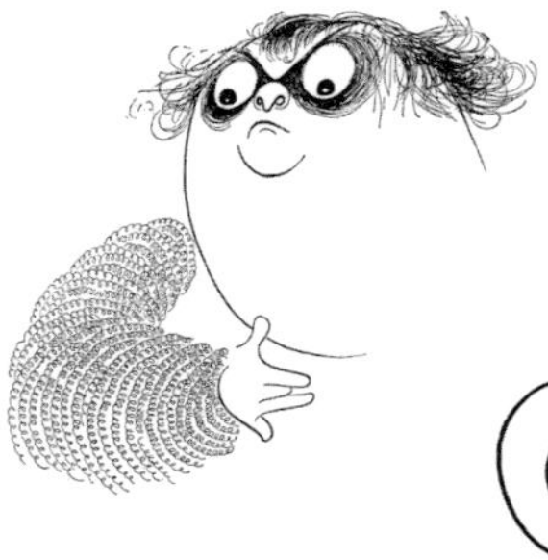

1962

*A Funny Thing
Happened on the Way
to the Forum*

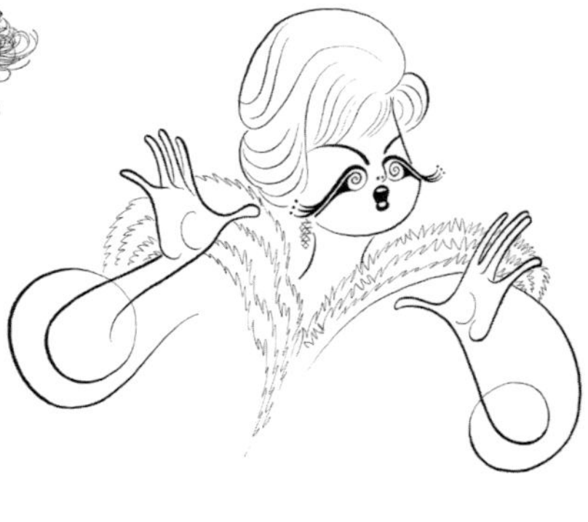

1964

Anyone Can Whistle

1974

Gypsy
(revival)

1976

*Pacific
Overtures*

1977

*Side by Side
by Sondheim*

1979

Sweeney Todd

1979

*The Madwoman
of Central
Park West* [2]

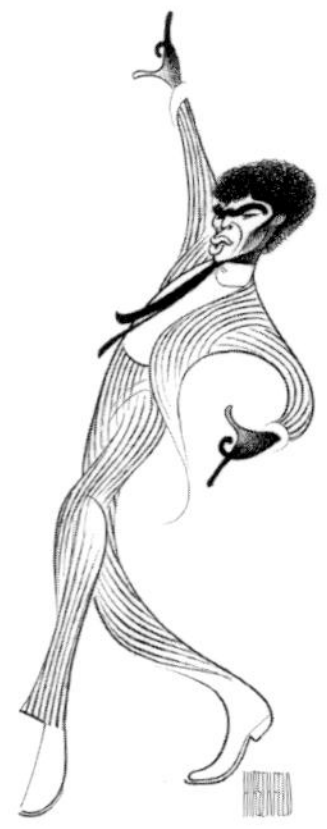

1980

West Side Story
(revival)

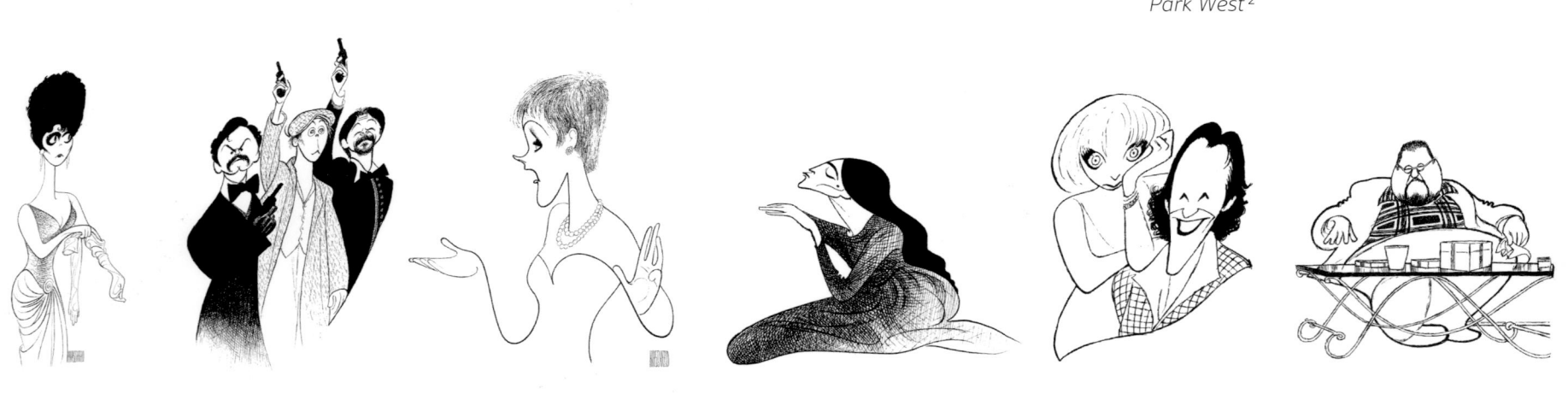

1989

Gypsy
(revival)

1991

Assassins

1993

Putting It Together

1994

Passion

1995

Company
(revival)

1996

*Getting Away
with Murder*

A TIMELINE

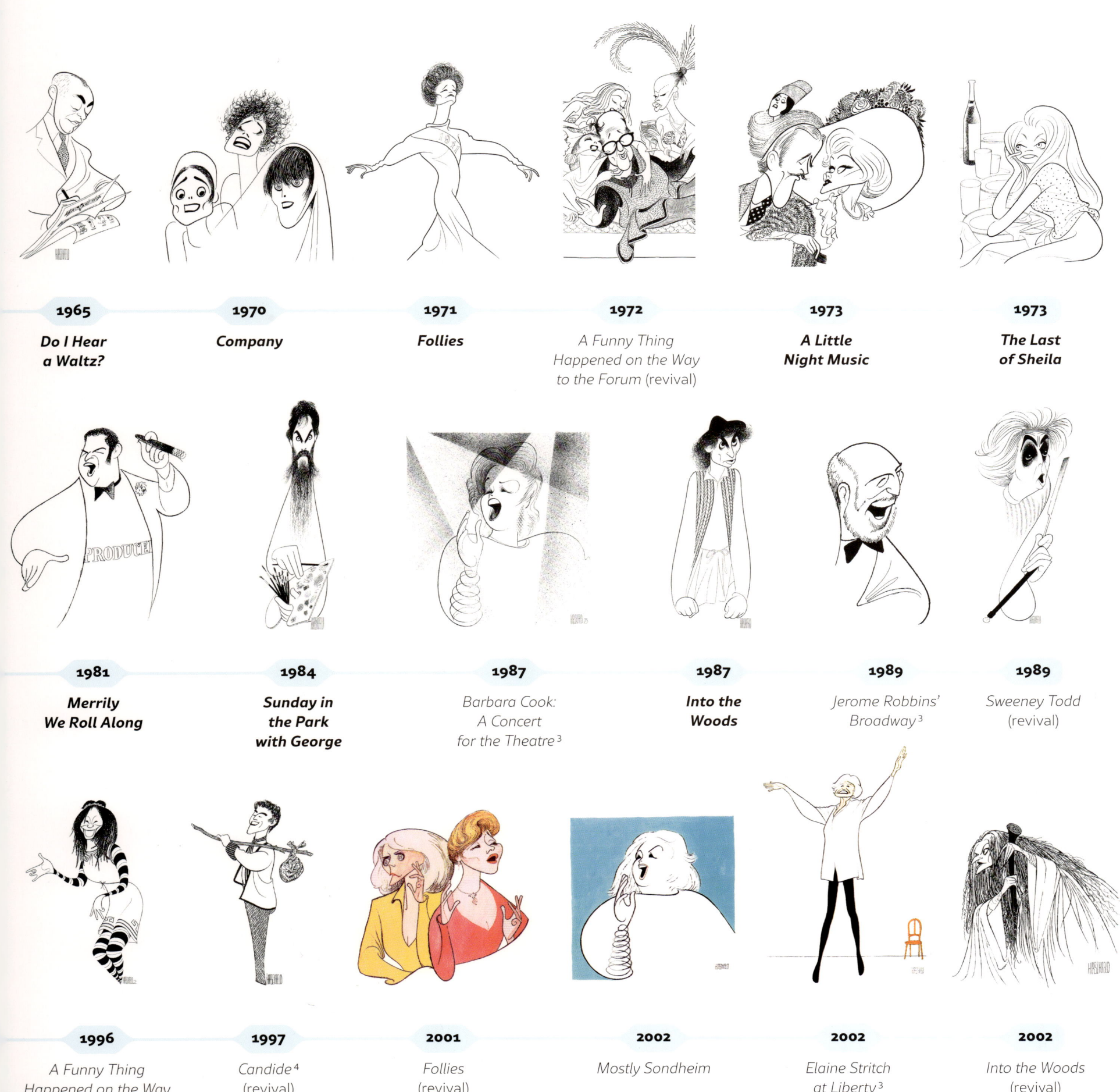

1965

Do I Hear a Waltz?

1970

Company

1971

Follies

1972

A Funny Thing Happened on the Way to the Forum (revival)

1973

A Little Night Music

1973

The Last of Sheila

1981

Merrily We Roll Along

1984

Sunday in the Park with George

1987

Barbara Cook: A Concert for the Theatre [3]

1987

Into the Woods

1989

Jerome Robbins' Broadway [3]

1989

Sweeney Todd (revival)

1996

A Funny Thing Happened on the Way to the Forum (revival)

1997

Candide [4] *(revival)*

2001

Follies (revival)

2002

Mostly Sondheim

2002

Elaine Stritch at Liberty [3]

2002

Into the Woods (revival)

Titles in **bold** are featured as posters in this book.   [1] Incidental music by Sondheim.   [2] Additional music by Sondheim.   [3] Songs by Sondheim.   [4] Additional lyrics by Sondheim.

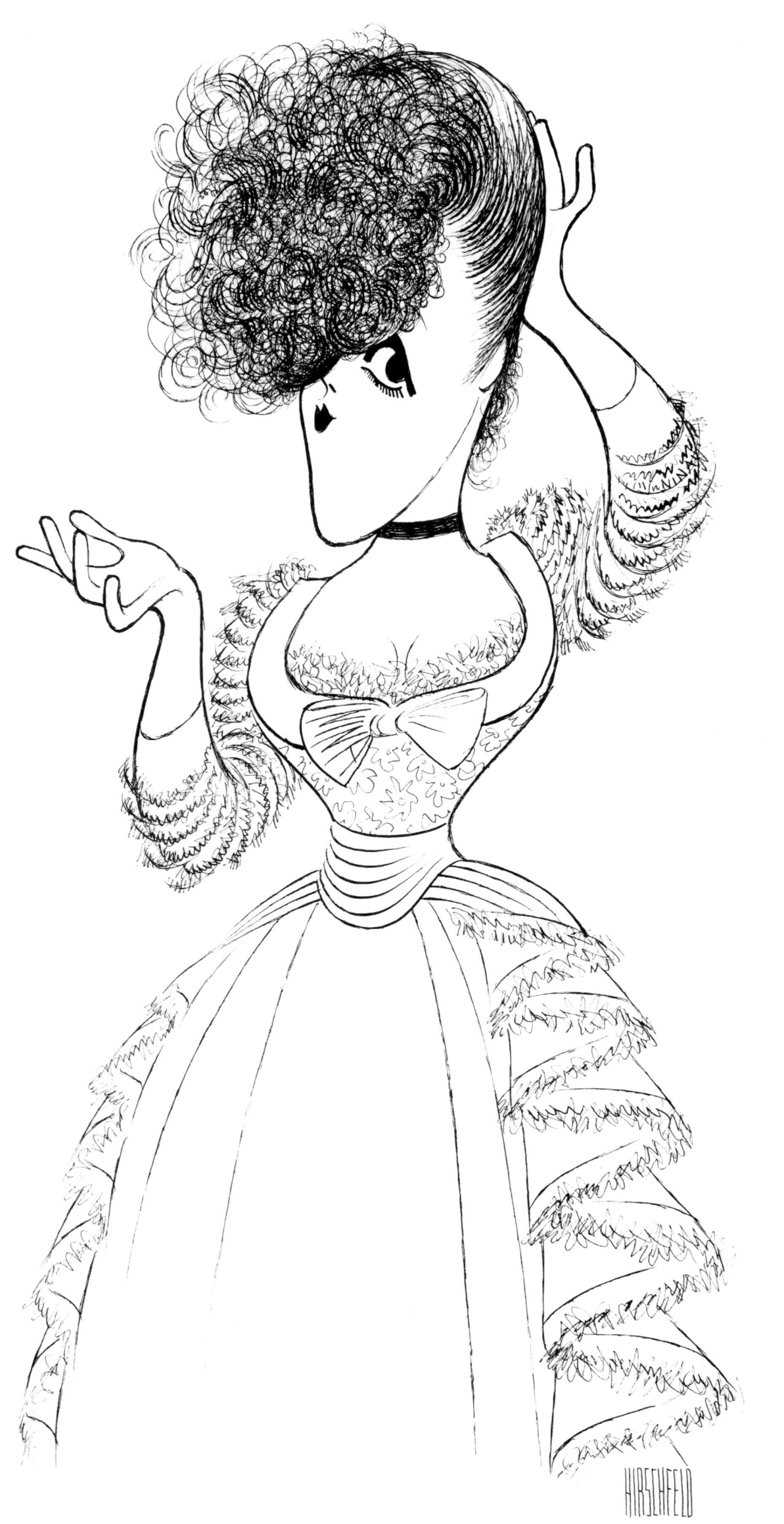

Introduction

HIRSCHFELD AND SONDHEIM . . . TWO ORIGINAL GENIUSES!

by Bernadette Peters

Hirschfeld's Sondheim is a magnificent collection of Al's wonderful drawings of Steve and his seminal artistic productions. Beginning in 1957, when Al drew his first Sondheim creation of *West Side Story*, and then chronicling Steve for another fifty years, these two giants helped to define the wonder of Broadway.

This keepsake treasure book is graced with fifty remarkable drawings (twenty-five as posters) spanning Steve's most acclaimed works. I can hardly think of a better way to memorialize Steve and his art other than actually watching his shows or listening to his songs. Al, in a single image, captures a memorable emotion, indelibly etching our hearts and memories with Steve's artistic contributions.

As I leaf through this special book, I recognize how privileged I have been to know and work with these two special men. I benefited greatly from their guidance in countless ways.

If you have never been drawn by Hirschfeld, I can tell you it's a treat because he captures your essence! When you see yourself for the first time, you're in for a little bit of a shock!

First, you love that he's drawn you, and second, you ask yourself: *Do I really look like that? Do other people look like that?! Are Angela's eyes really that big?*

But look at the drawing he did of himself. With just a few lines, it's the essence he makes you see, and that was what he captured!

We all loved waiting for the Sunday paper, anticipating Al's next famous caricature. Growing up, many of us collected them, hanging the newspaper on our walls. I know Steve loved them too. He also prized his collection of Al's original creations. They were pure theater.

Steve and Al both dealt with lines and dots to create their mesmerizing magic. Al's dots and lines and squiggles turned into a lively picture of people singing, dancing, and acting on the page right before you. You can feel the energy!

Steve's lines and dots and squiggles created musical phrases that would turn into a song with an idea and emotional theme that would surprise you because they hit you in a startling way.

Notably, if you look at the drawing of Steve, you will notice that Al drew his trademark "NINAs" coming out of Steve's pen and onto the music. Yes, his world-renowned NINAs. For those who are not familiar with them, Al would write his daughter's name hidden within the hem of a skirt or the ruffle of a blouse or in someone's wrinkles. He would then put the number of NINAs next to his signature. He memorialized in each drawing his love for his daughter and also created a little game, indeed a national obsession, for his adoring audience as they searched for the right answer. How many NINAs were in each sketch, and could you find every last one of them? Needless to say, each of his puzzles was no easy task to solve!

I suggest that when you open this wonderful book and look at Al's caricatures, you also listen to the music from Steve's shows. You will get an idea of what Al was feeling while he was in the audience experiencing the show as he was sketching.

Thankfully, we now have this special book to memorialize two great theater giants and their amazing artistic talents as we celebrate a wonderful era of Broadway.

Bernadette Peters in *Sunday in the Park with George*
Ink on board, 1984
First published in the *New York Times*, June 8, 1984

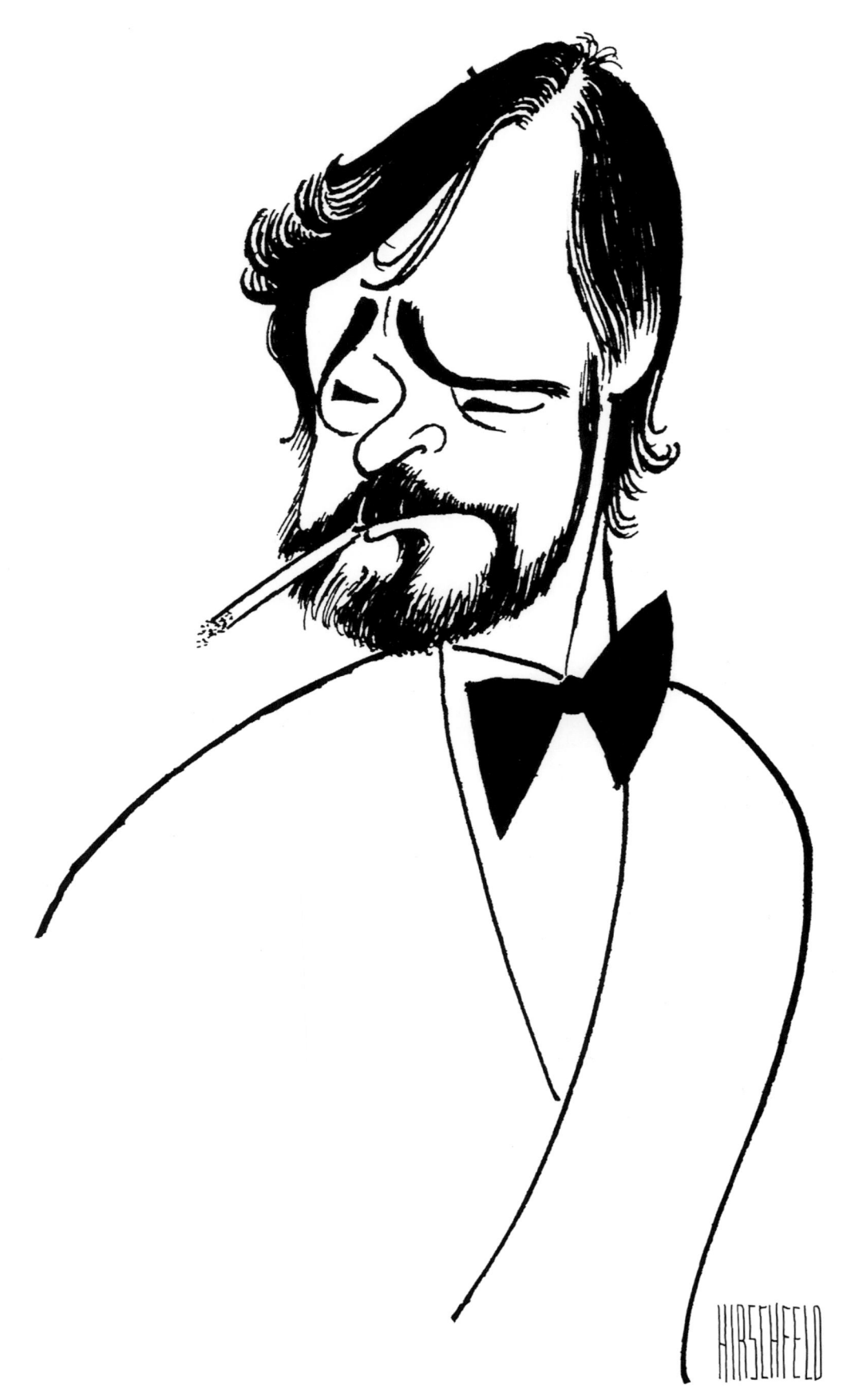

THESE HIRSCHFELD DRAWINGS CAPTURE SONDHEIM'S SHOWS BETTER THAN ANY PHOTO

by Ben Brantley

Ever since Stephen Sondheim died, certain images have been flaring in my head, so insistently that I have to catch my breath. They come with sound, of course—they're inseparable from the music that feeds them. And they possess those heightened but elusive qualities that only firsthand memory confers.

Alexis Smith, in red spangles, winking at the audience as she launches into an irresistibly rhymed confession of a divided self in *Follies* (from 1971, and my first Broadway show). Angela Lansbury and Len Cariou rising through the stage floor as waxwork corpses, singing one of the most chilling reprises in Broadway musical history, in *Sweeney Todd* (1979). Mandy Patinkin finding anguished, atomic energy in a painter's obsessive quest to render a hat on canvas in *Sunday in the Park with George* (1984).

Strangely, the visuals that come closest to evoking such moments are not the photos or videos of performances but, instead, black lines—and whorls and swirls and loops—on white paper. They are the work of the great theater caricaturist Al Hirschfeld, whose drawings of all things theatrical in the Sunday *New York Times* have entranced me since I was a child in North Carolina. Even then, these pictures seemed to breathe and move in a way the photographs in the same pages never could. Somehow, they even smelled like Broadway to me.

Recently, I've been looking through his drawings of works by Sondheim, who seems particularly to have engaged and inspired Hirschfeld. They span the decades, from *West Side Story* and *Gypsy* (for which Sondheim wrote the lyrics) in the 1950s to *Passion*, Sondheim's last new show on Broadway, from 1994. In these drawings, I have found something like a past-recapturing, Proustian madeleine, made of ink instead of flour and sugar.

These seemingly simple pen strokes—and the ellipsis of the white space, which your own, happily collaborative mind fills

in—are anything but static. They tremble with energy, tension, and, above all, *character*, as it is conjured in real time on a stage.

Hirschfeld always said he would rather be called a "characterist" than a caricaturist. His illustrations of Sondheim, the most complex character portraitist in the Broadway songbook, make you understand why. Caricatures are a shorthand for the physical traits that make stars distinctive: Angela Lansbury's immense Tweety Bird eyes, for example, or Bernadette Peters's Cupid's bow mouth.

Hirschfeld nails such elements of physiognomy. He also endows them with the exciting emotional temperature that heats up every Sondheim song. The Lansbury he draws as the corrupt mayor Cora Hoover Hooper of *Anyone Can Whistle* (1964) and as the cannibal pie-maker Mrs. Lovett in *Sweeney Todd* are recognizably the same woman.

But you can also feel how Lansbury physically and psychically inhabits these roles in the slope and size of her shoulders, in the focus in those saucer eyes—manically mesmerized as Cora, fretful and eager as Mrs. Lovett. After staring at the *Whistle* illustration, in which Cora's outsize ambition dwarfs the frame, I could swear that I saw that production, though I couldn't possibly have.

Consider Hirschfeld's Joanna Gleason, restless and leery as the Baker's Wife in *Into the Woods*. Or Patinkin and Peters—he all penetrating angles, and she, self-contained curves—as the incompatibly in-love artist and model of *Sunday*. Or Donna Murphy, as implacable and demanding as some Assyrian god, as the sickly, love-consumed Fosca in *Passion*.

The diversity and scope of tone and substance embodied in drawings, in all their gleeful concentration of energy, make you understand why a Sondheim character remains a holy grail for singing actors.

Those figures have included the inhabitants of two very different Sondheim shows, which shared a season just after his death and attest to his dizzying range. *Assassins* (a dark show that left

Stephen Sondheim
Detail of American Musical Theatre mural, 1999

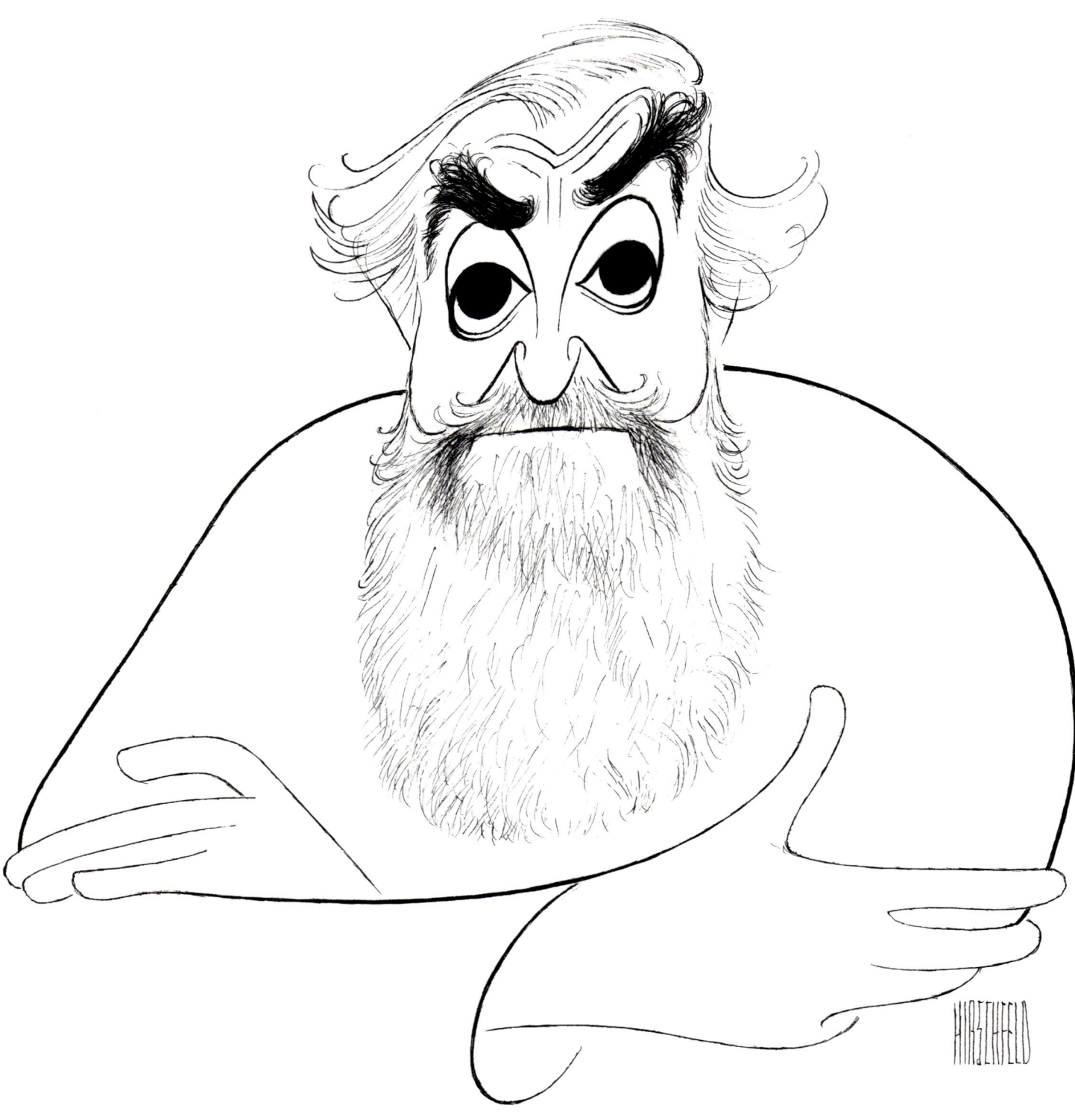

me sleepless after I first saw it Off-Broadway in 1991), at the Classic Stage Company, and *Company*, Sondheim's breakthrough work from 1970 about being single in a world of Manhattan marrieds.

The director Marianne Elliot's gender-reversed production of *Company* was the more radically reconceived. I had caught its first incarnation in London, and anticipating its arrival on Broadway, I found an odd and comforting appropriateness to this period of mourning Sondheim in Hirschfeld's sketch of the original show.

Hirschfeld portrays the show's leading man, the ambivalent bachelor Bobby (Dean Jones), surrounded by and submerged in the tantalizing phantoms of the women in his life. You get the impression that Bobby will never be free of their presences. Typically, Bobby appears to regard this life sentence with both regret and pleasure. Me, I feel only pleasure—and so much gratitude—at the prospect of being haunted for the rest of my life by the ghosts of Sondheim performances past.

Ben Brantley served as the chief theater critic for the *New York Times* from 1996 to 2017, and as co–chief theater critic from 2017 to 2020. He wrote more than 2,500 reviews over twenty-seven years beginning in 1993, filing regularly from London as well as New York. He retired from regular reviewing in 2020. This appreciation of Stephen Sondheim, who passed away on November 26, 2021, originally appeared in the *New York Times* on December 9, 2021, and is reprinted with permission.

Self-portrait, 1985

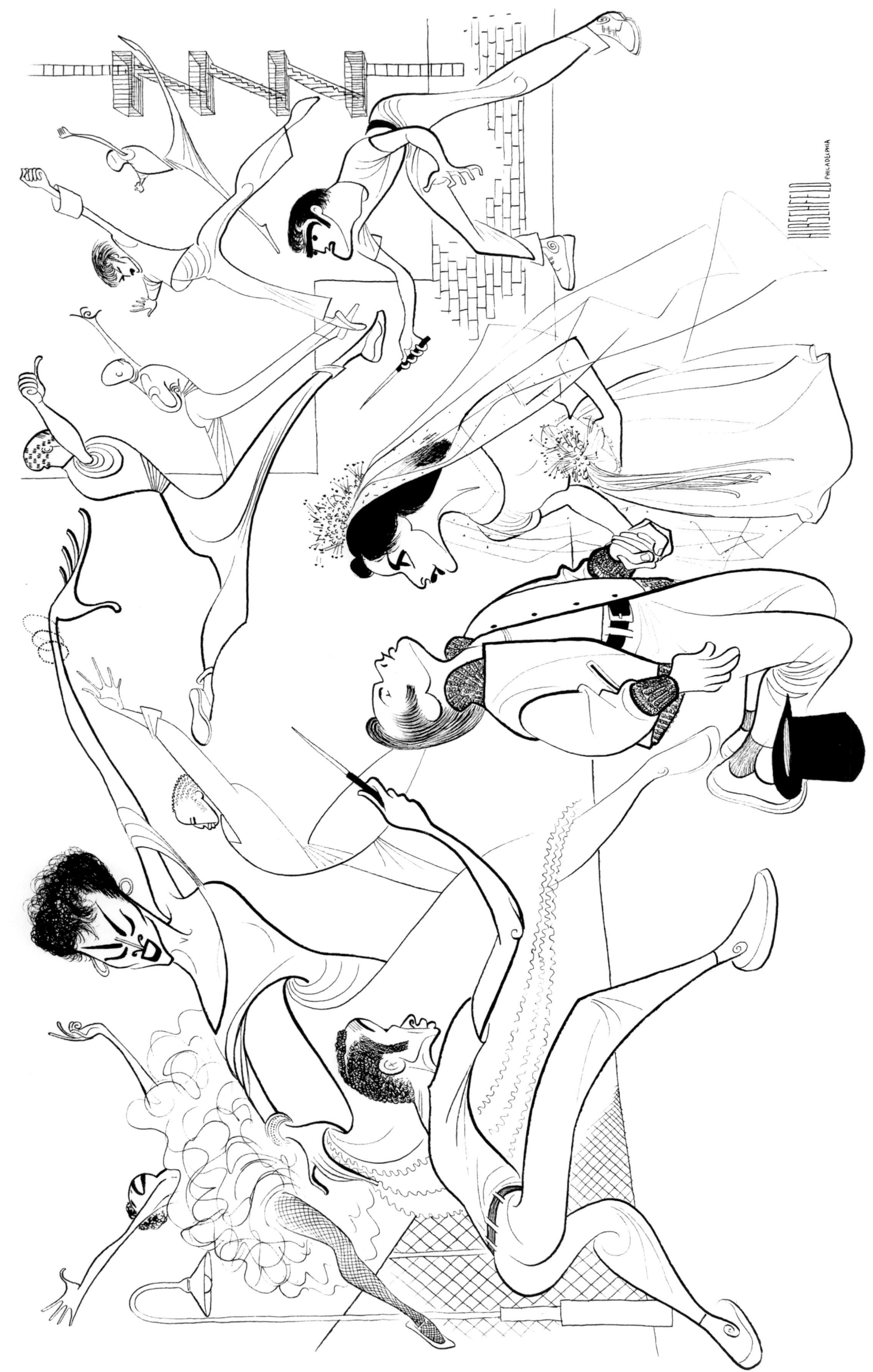

WEST SIDE STORY

LEFT TO RIGHT: Ken Leroy, Chita Rivera, Larry Kert, Carol Lawrence, and Mickey Calin

Ink on board, 1957

First published in the *New York Times*, September 22, 1957

Lyrics by Stephen Sondheim; music by Leonard Bernstein; book by Arthur Laurents

OPENING DATE: September 26, 1957
CLOSING DATE: June 27, 1959
PERFORMANCES ON BROADWAY: 732

Nominated for six Tony Awards, it won two:
◦ Best Scenic Design: Oliver Smith
◦ Best Choreography: Jerome Robbins

Hirschfeld sketching during a rehearsal, c. 1960

Although Sondheim had one song in a play on Broadway in 1956, his real Broadway debut was supplying lyrics to *West Side Story*, which was conceived, directed, and choreographed by Jerome Robbins. The creative team and the show's producer, Harold Prince, would remain some of his most regular and significant collaborators throughout Sondheim's career. The show's focus on social problems and its tragic theme, its emphasis on story-telling through dance and sophisticated music, marked a turning point in musical theater.

Hirschfeld made his preliminary sketches for the production in Philadelphia during the show's out-of-town tryout (noted alongside his signature), and his finished drawing appeared the Sunday before the show opened on Broadway. Virtually all of Hirschfeld's theater drawings in the *New York Times* appeared the Sunday before a show opened. His works, for most of his career, were stand-alone features, rather than illustrations for articles or reviews. His drawings were as much a part of the Broadway experience as opening night, and more people saw his drawings of these shows than saw the shows themselves.

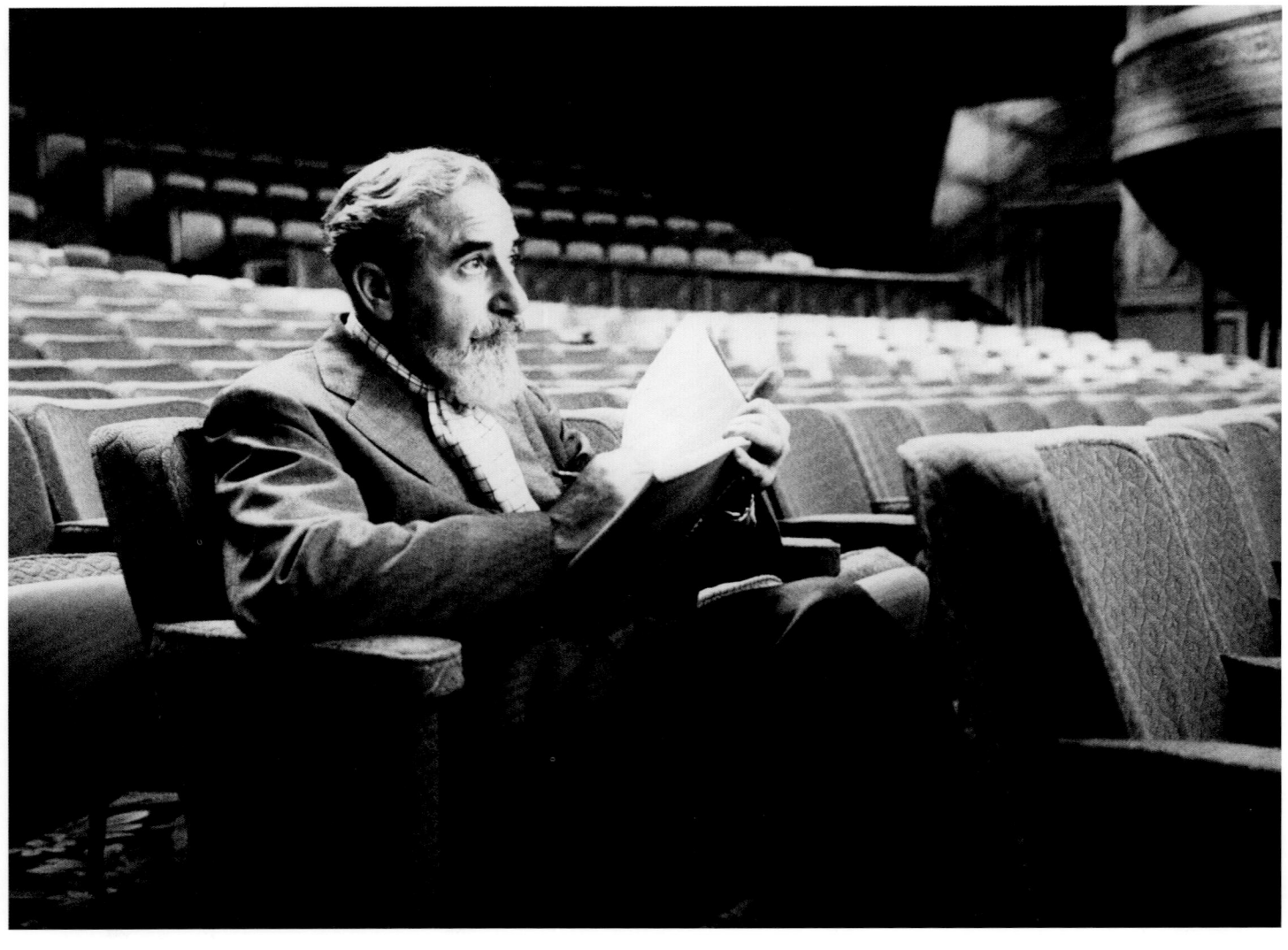

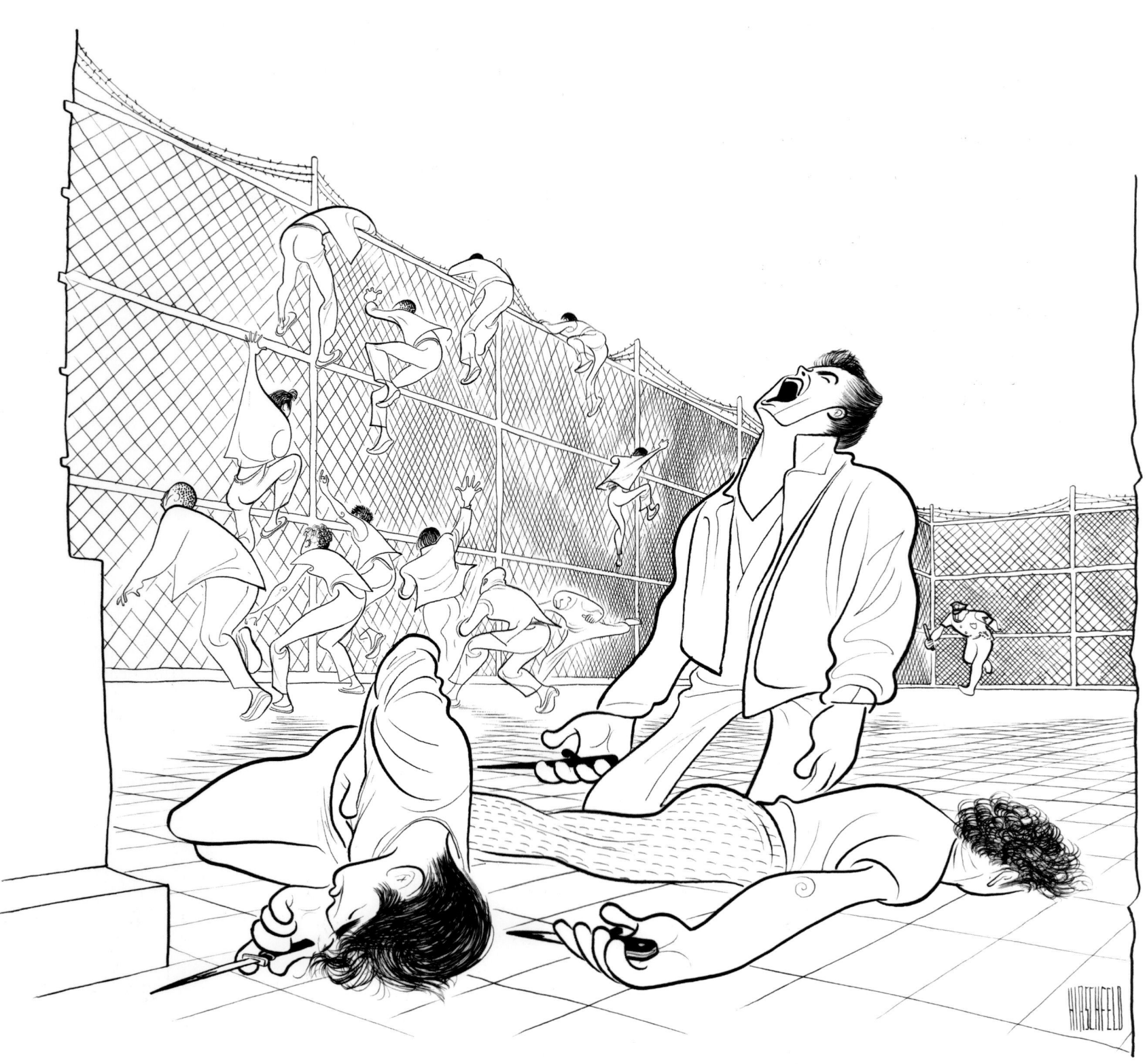

WEST SIDE STORY (film adaptation)

LEFT TO RIGHT: George Chakiris, Richard Beymer, and Russ Tamblyn

Ink on board, 1961

Drawn to promote the film by United Artists, this image appeared in publications all over the United States and Europe.

Nominated for eleven Academy Awards, it won ten— a record for a musical film:
- Best Picture
- Best Actor in a Supporting Role: George Chakiris
- Best Actress in a Supporting Role: Rita Moreno
- Best Director: Robert Wise and Jerome Robbins (the first time the Best Director award was shared)
- Best Music, Scoring of a Musical Picture
- Best Cinematography, Color: Daniel L. Fapp
- Best Art Direction-Set Decoration, Color: Boris Leven and Victor A. Gangelin
- Best Costume Design, Color: Irene Sharaff
- Best Sound: Todd-AO and Samuel Goldwyn Studio Sound Departments
- Best Film Editing: Thomas Stanford

This adaptation of the Broadway musical was Sondheim's first film credit. Released through United Artists on October 18, 1961, the film received rave reviews from both critics and audiences and became the highest-grossing film of 1961. Considered by many to be one of the greatest film musicals, *West Side Story* was selected in 1997 by the Library of Congress for preservation in the United States National Film Registry for being "culturally, historically, or aesthetically significant."

Hirschfeld visited the set on Tenth Avenue in New York and created three drawings of the film. The first drawing shows a scene of Robert Wise and Jerry Robbins auditioning dancers on Tenth Avenue. The second was a "cast drawing," showing the principals of the cast from multiple perspectives. And finally, this dramatic scene. Hirschfeld chose what was the Act One finale when Tony, who tries to stop a rumble between the two gangs, kills Bernardo, the Sharks' leader, after he kills Riff, the Jets' leader, and a melee ensues. Everyone flees when the police sirens are heard, leaving behind dead members of both gangs.

Robbins purchased this drawing when it was completed, and it hung in his home for the rest of his life. It is now in the collection of Harvard University.

On the set of *West Side Story* as (left to right) Robert Wise and Jerome Robbins screen-test the dancers, 1960

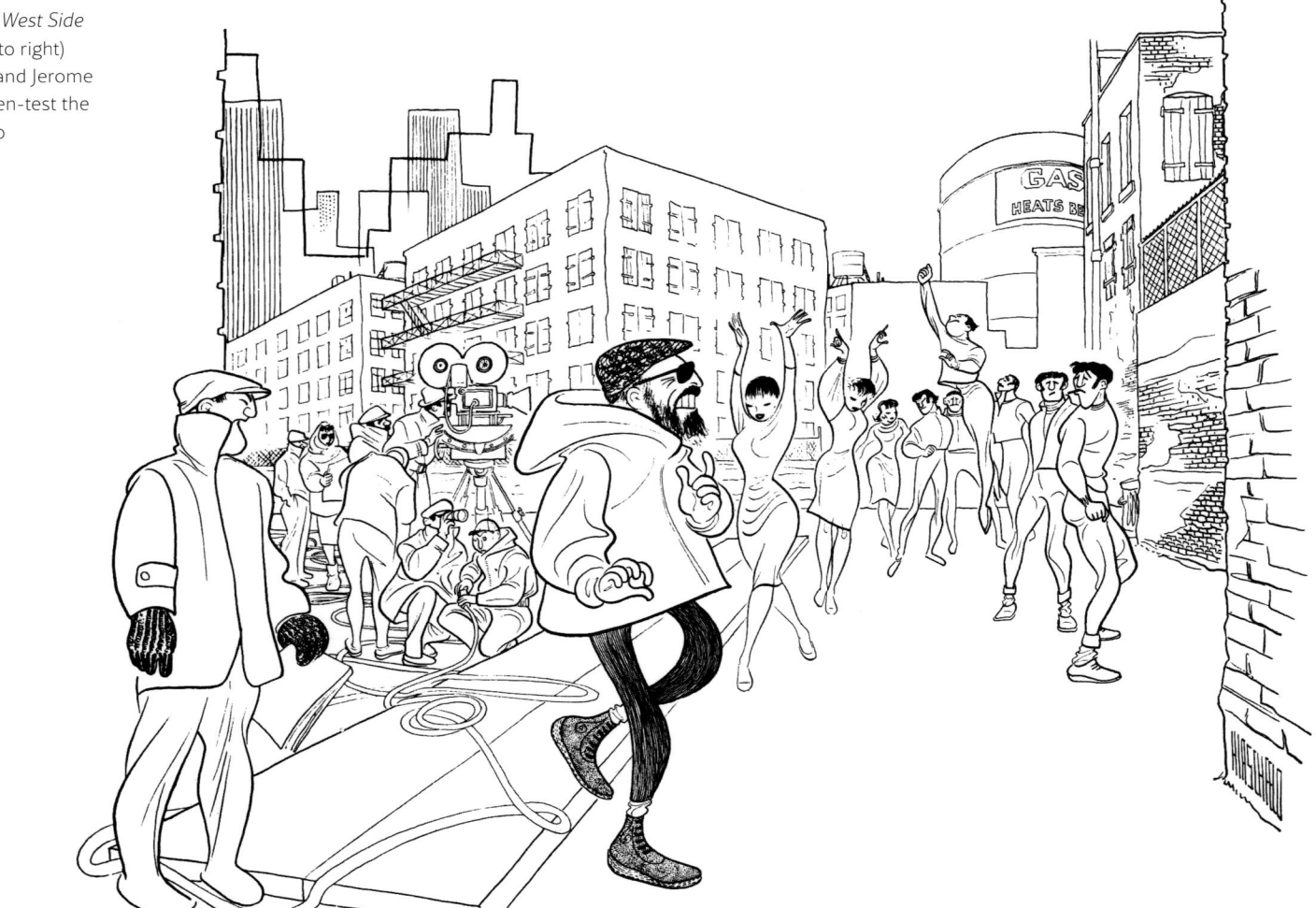

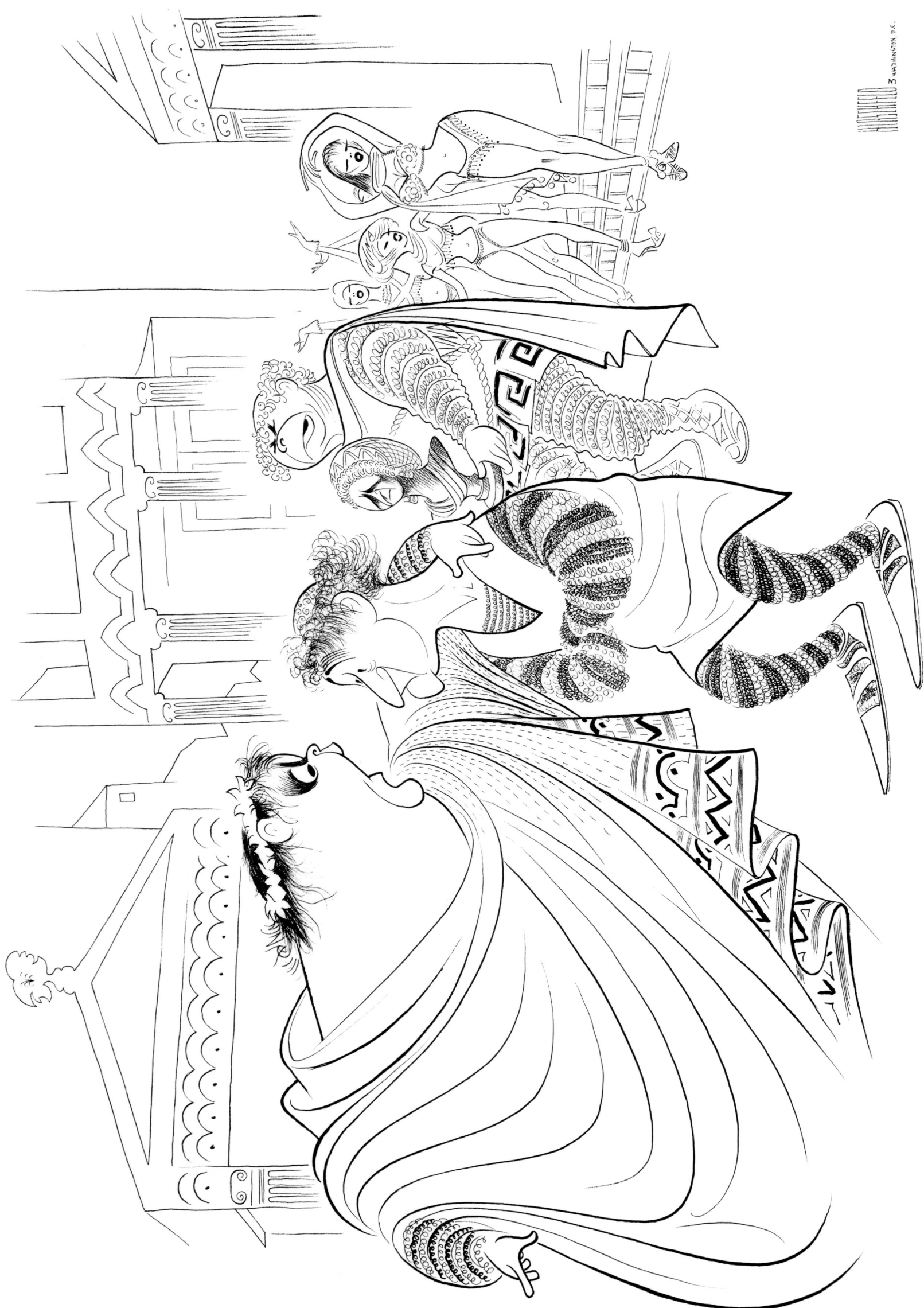

A FUNNY THING HAPPENED ON THE WAY TO THE FORUM

LEFT TO RIGHT: Zero Mostel, Jack Gilford, and David Burns

Ink on board, 1962

First published in the *New York Times*, May 6, 1962

Music and lyrics by Stephen Sondheim;
book by Burt Shevelove and Larry Gelbart

OPENING DATE: May 8, 1962
CLOSING DATE: August 29, 1964
PERFORMANCES ON BROADWAY: 964

Nominated for eight Tony Awards, it won six:
◦ Best Musical
◦ Best Author of a Musical
◦ Best Actor in a Musical: Zero Mostel
◦ Best Featured Actor in a Musical: David Burns
◦ Best Direction of a Musical: George Abbott
◦ Best Producer of a Musical: Harold Prince

A Funny Thing Happened
on the Way to the Forum (revival)
LEFT TO RIGHT: Larry Blyden and Phil Silvers, 1972

Hirschfeld saw *A Funny Thing Happened on the Way to the Forum* in its tryout in Washington, DC, where he made his preliminary sketches. For the artist, the "exploded ventricle" that was Zero Mostel was the comic engine of the show. Hirschfeld loved performers who "don't close a door, they slam it." He had met Mostel when the actor was still a painter named Sam who would occasionally stop by Hirschfeld's Sheridan Square studio in the West Village and make him laugh. Hirschfeld suggested Mostel to Barney Josephson at New York's first integrated club, Café Society. Josephson was looking for someone to warm up the audience for his headliner. The gig gave Mostel a new name, Zero, and a new career, as he was soon hired for radio, Broadway, and Hollywood.

A Funny Thing Happened on the Way to the Forum was Sondheim's first success as both a lyricist and a composer. He had been a frustrated composer whose first show, *Saturday Night* (1954), was canceled when its producer died before raising enough money. Sondheim had been rejected by Ethel Merman to write the music for *Gypsy* in 1959 because she wanted someone with "experience." *A Funny Thing . . .* showed that Sondheim could write both music and lyrics successfully, and he would later consider the show the "desert island musical" of his own works.

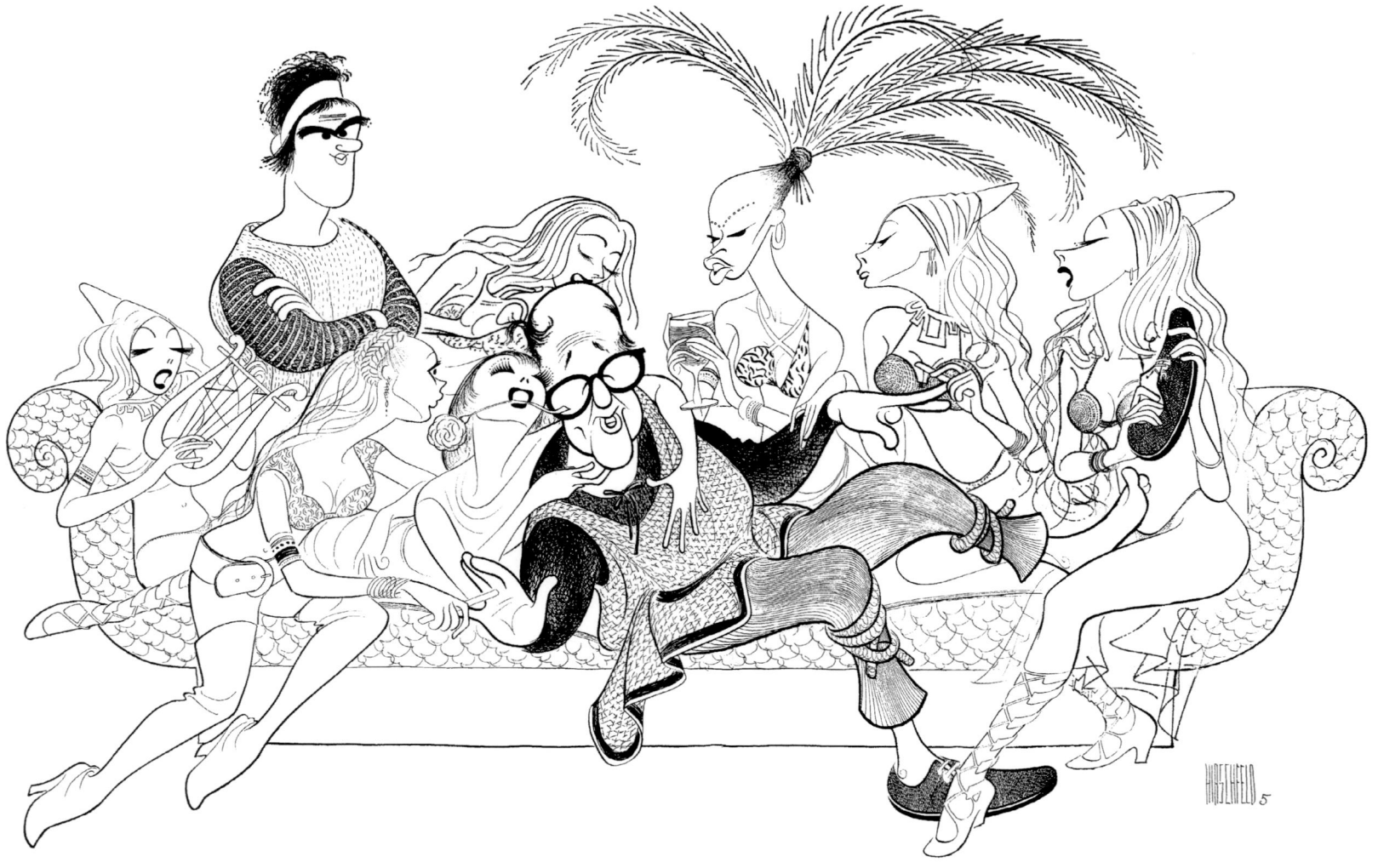

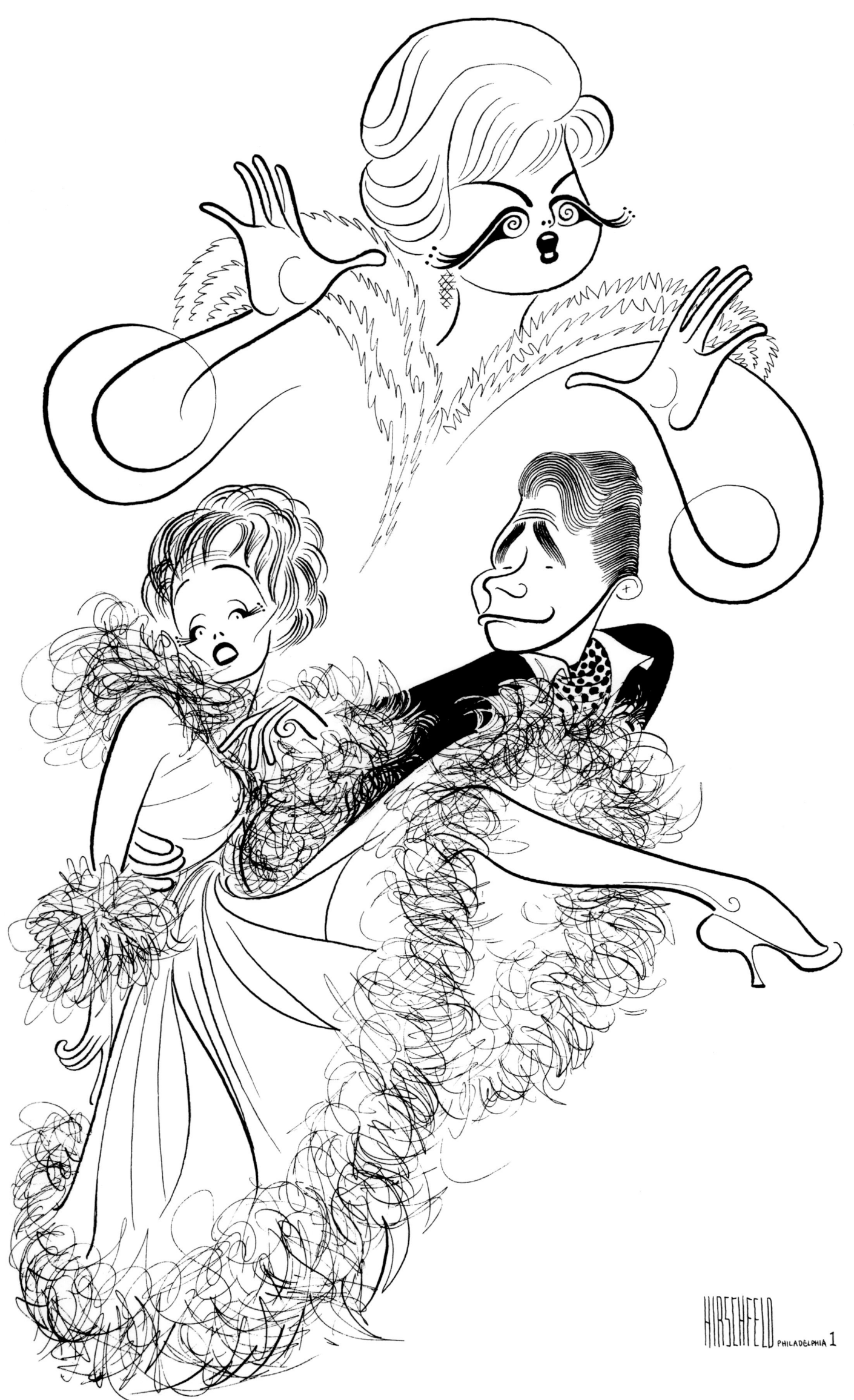

ANYONE CAN WHISTLE

LEFT TO RIGHT: Lee Remick, Angela Lansbury, and Harry Guardino

Ink on board, 1964

First published in the *New York Times*, March 29, 1964

Music and lyrics by Stephen Sondheim; book by Arthur Laurents

OPENING DATE: April 4, 1964
CLOSING DATE: April 11, 1964
PERFORMANCES ON BROADWAY: 9

Nominated for one Tony Award:
○ Best Choreography: Herbert Ross

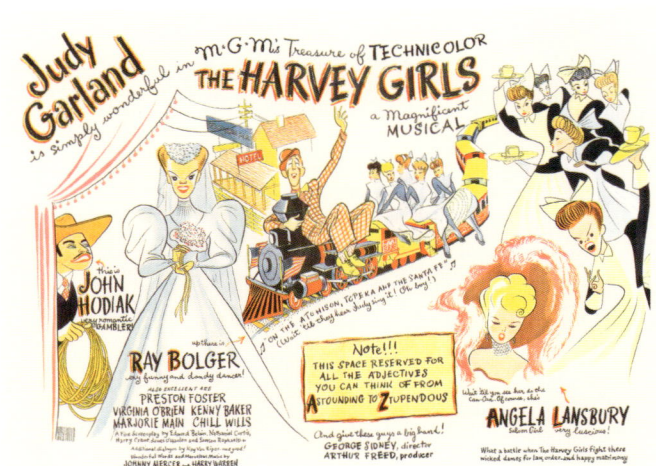

Shortly before Oscar Hammerstein, Sondheim's mentor, died in 1960, he told a mutual friend that despite Sondheim's first three Broadway shows being hits, "Steve won't really be a member of the working theater until he has a flop." As with most lessons Hammerstein taught Sondheim, this one turned out to also be true. *Anyone Can Whistle* was described in the caption of this drawing in the *Times* as "a musical that takes a satiric view of the conformity and the general madness of our world." The public turned out not to be interested in what the composer described as "one of the first absurdist (with commercial intentions) musicals." It ran for only one week.

Hirschfeld caught the star-crossed production in its Philadelphia tryout. He had drawn Angela Lansbury seven times over nearly twenty years in films for MGM and United Artists, including two years earlier in her Oscar–nominated role as the power-hungry Eleanor Iselin in *The Manchurian Candidate*. Here, she played another corrupt character: the crooked mayor of an economically depressed town who decides to create a fake miracle to attract tourists. The tourists come but soon intermingle with inmates of an asylum for "nonconformists." As Sondheim would later write, "Farcical complications ensue."

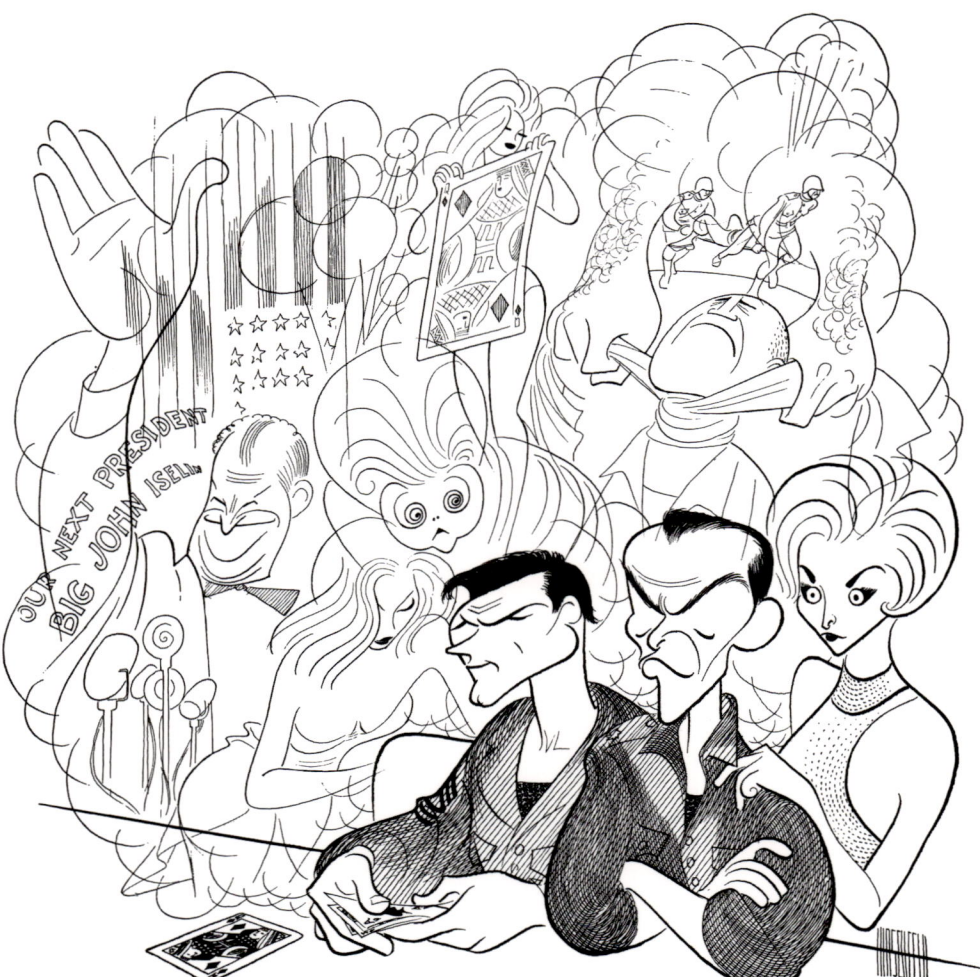

ABOVE
The Harvey Girls
LEFT TO RIGHT: John Hodiak, Judy Garland, Ray Bolger, and Angela Lansbury, 1946

LEFT
The Manchurian Candidate
LEFT TO RIGHT: James Gregory, Angela Lansbury, Laurence Harvey, Frank Sinatra, and Leslie Parrish, 1962

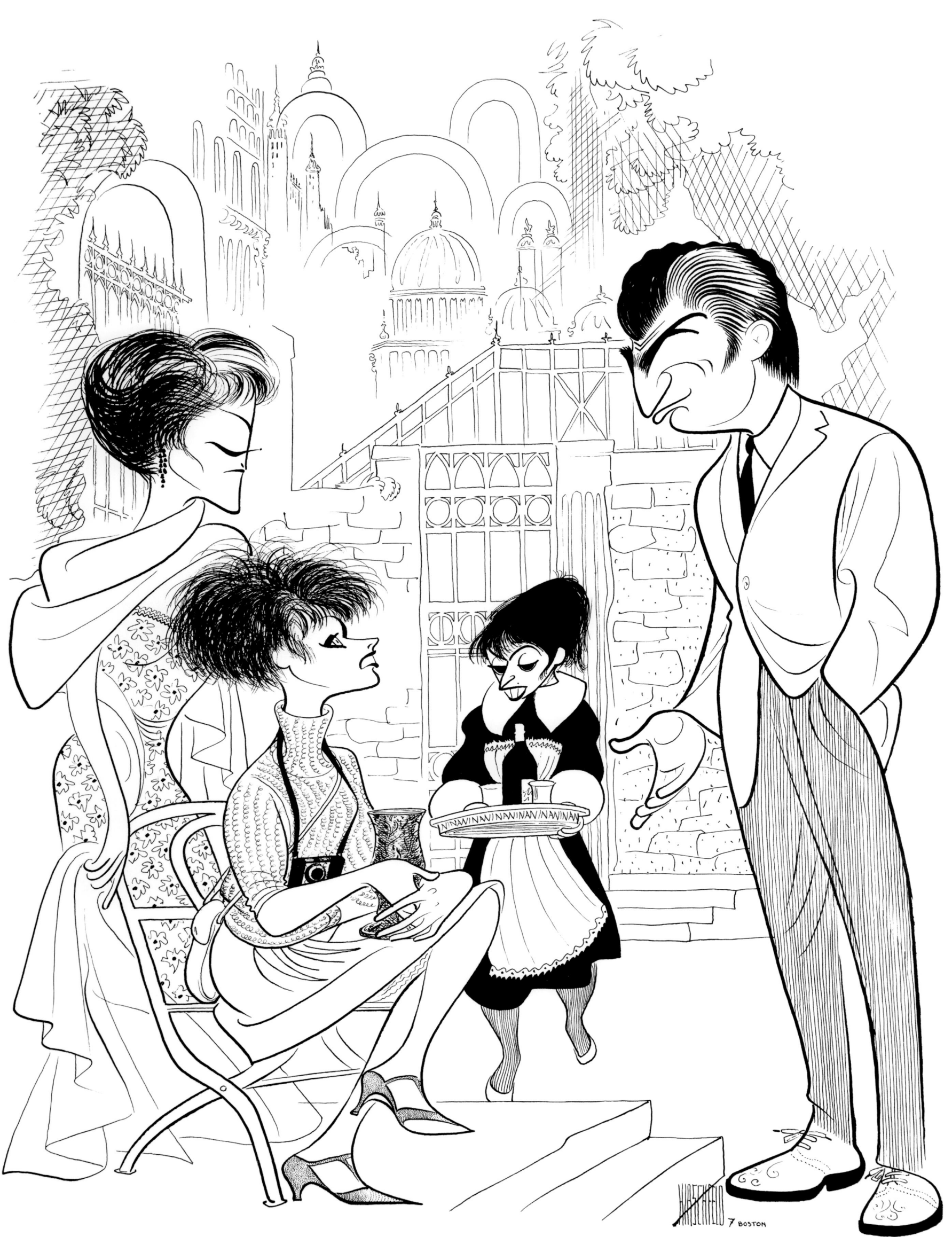

DO I HEAR A WALTZ?

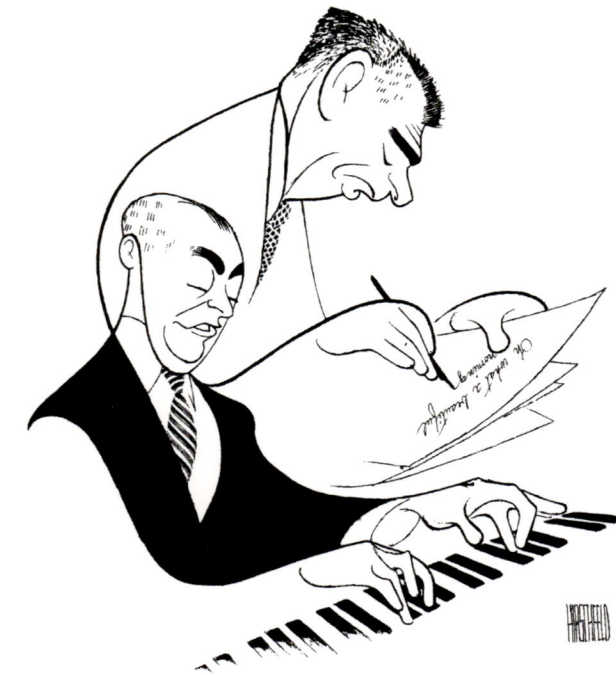

LEFT TO RIGHT: Carol Bruce, Elizabeth Allen, Fleury D'Antonakis, and Sergio Franchi

Ink on board, 1965

First published in the *New York Times*, March 14, 1965

Lyrics by Stephen Sondheim; music by Richard Rodgers; book by Arthur Laurents, based on his play *The Time of the Cuckoo*

OPENING DATE: May 18, 1965
CLOSING DATE: September 25, 1965
PERFORMANCES ON BROADWAY: 220

Nominated for three Tony Awards:
- Best Composer and Lyricist
- Best Actress: Elizabeth Allen
- Best Scenic Design: Beni Montresor

Hirschfeld's career was so long that his professional life predated Rodgers and Hart's first full show on Broadway. He was there at one of the first previews of the first Rodgers and Hammerstein collaboration, *Away We Go!* (which was soon retitled *Oklahoma!*). So it was natural to draw Rodgers's first and only collaboration with Hammerstein's protégé Sondheim.

On Hammerstein's deathbed, he encouraged the young composer to agree to supply lyrics to Rodgers if he ever asked. While Rodgers did send Sondheim several scripts in the aftermath of Hammerstein's passing, none interested Sondheim until Arthur Laurents suggested working with Rodgers on a musical adaptation of his successful 1952 play *The Time of the Cuckoo*. Laurents had originally approached Hammerstein in 1958 to have him and Rodgers adapt his play, but the film version, *Summertime*, starring Katharine Hepburn and directed by David Lean, had been recently released, and Hammerstein thought they should wait. Hammerstein died a little more than a year later. The combination of working again with Laurents and the opportunity to honor a promise to his mentor, as well as the likely opportunity to make money, led Sondheim to agree to collaborate with Rodgers on the songs.

Unfortunately, Sondheim found Rodgers too rigid in his thinking, and a mostly functioning alcoholic. Rodgers refused to change any music once it was written and would eventually become paranoid, thinking Sondheim and Laurents were scheming against him. The show was a modest hit, but it convinced Sondheim he should never work on anything again unless he felt passionate about it.

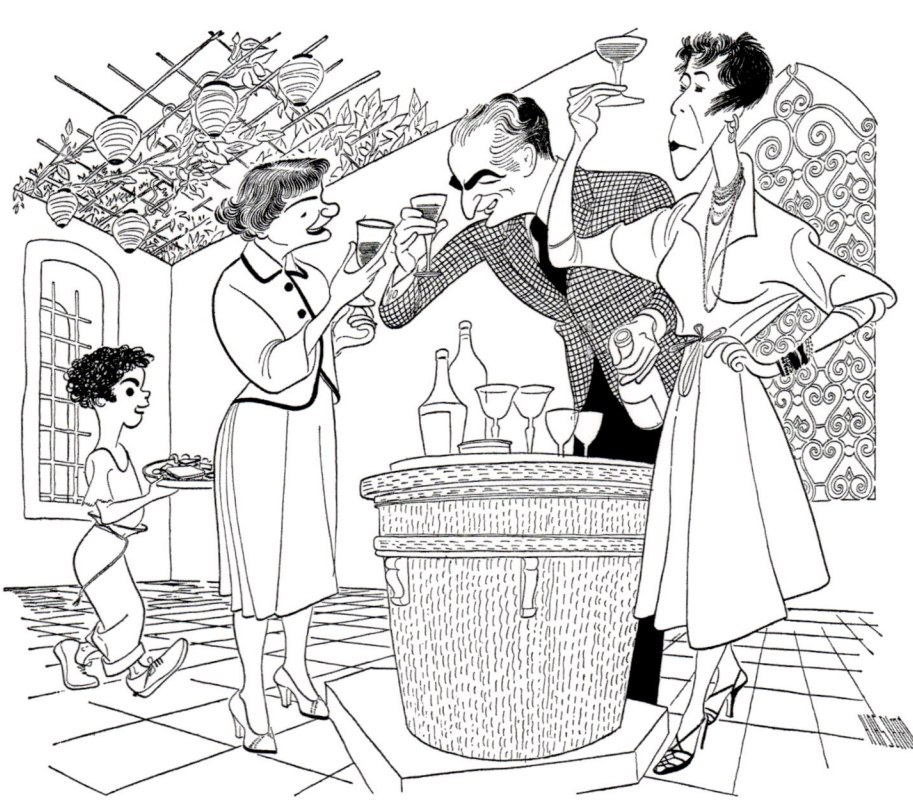

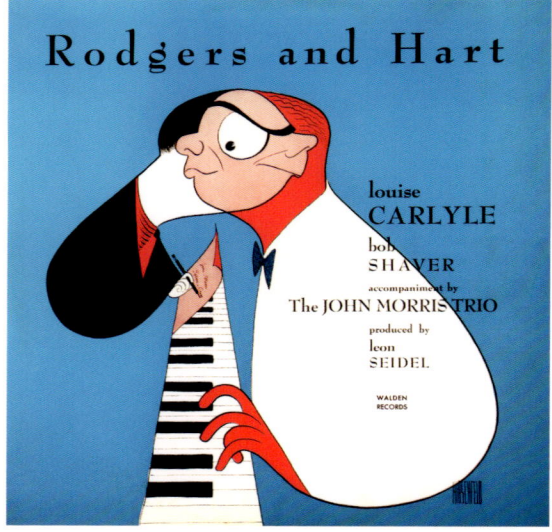

LEFT
The Time of the Cuckoo

LEFT TO RIGHT: Jose Perez, Shirley Booth, Dino Di Luca, and Lydia St. Clair, 1952

TOP
LEFT TO RIGHT:
Richard Rodgers and Oscar Hammerstein, 1993

ABOVE
Richard Rodgers and Lorenz Hart, album cover for Walden Records, 1953

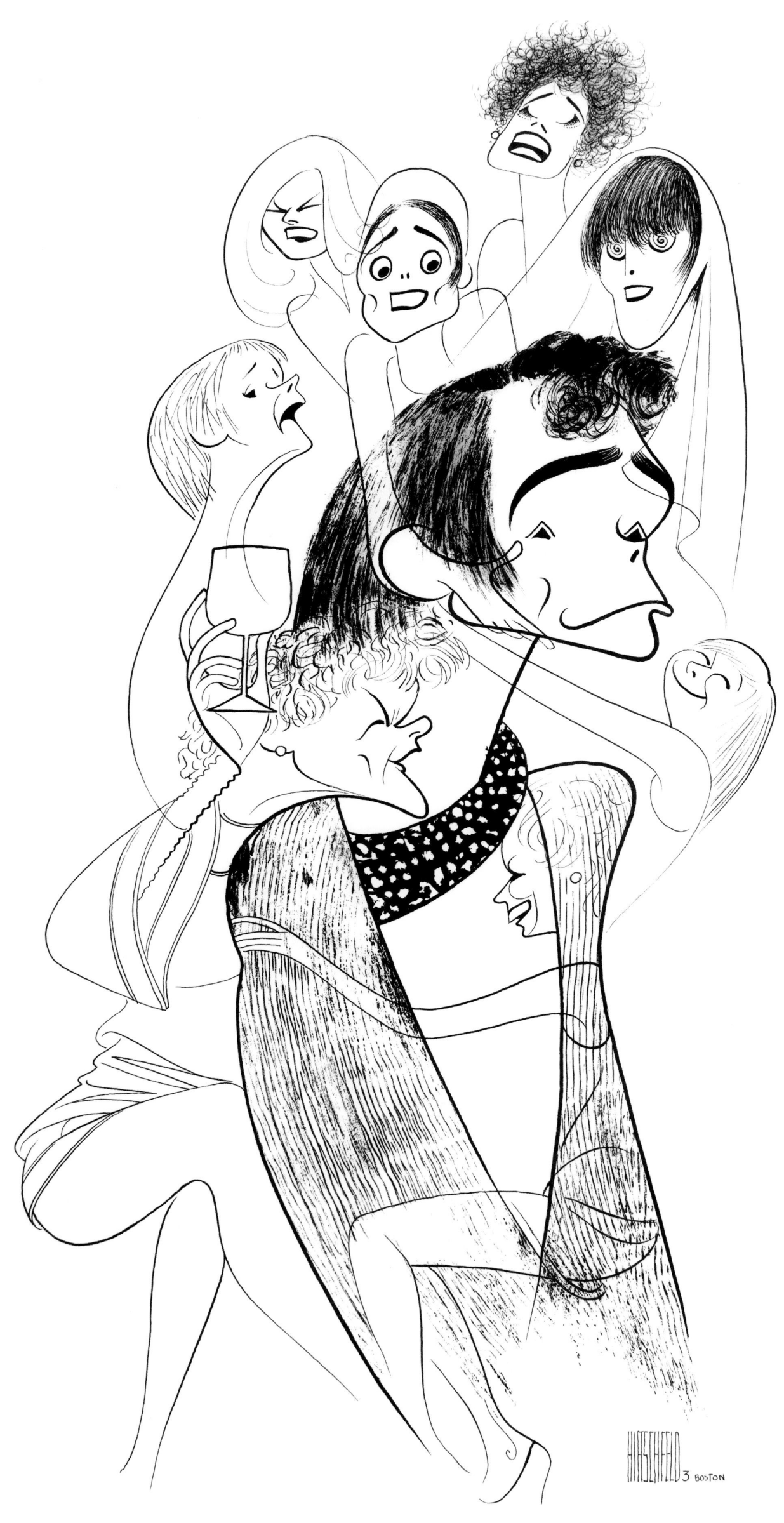

COMPANY

Dean Jones surrounded by the actresses who play the women in his life (CLOCKWISE FROM BOTTOM LEFT): Elaine Stritch, Barbara Barrie, Teri Ralston, Susan Browning, Donna McKechnie, Beth Howland, Pamela Myers, and Merle Louise

Ink on board, 1970

First published in the *New York Times*, April 26, 1970

Music and lyrics by Stephen Sondheim; book by George Furth

OPENING DATE: April 26, 1970
CLOSING DATE: January 1, 1972
PERFORMANCES ON BROADWAY: 705

Nominated for fifteen Tony Awards, it won six:
- Best Musical
- Best Book of a Musical
- Best Original Score
- Best Lyrics
- Best Direction of a Musical: Harold Prince
- Best Scenic Design: Boris Aronson

Company began as a group of eleven one-act plays by George Furth, an actor who turned to playwrighting at the suggestion of his therapist. After producer/director Harold Prince read the collection, he suggested the material would make a good musical. For Sondheim, the difficulty in transmuting the plays into a unifying musical about the relationships between couples seemed impossible to solve, which made it "irresistible" to the composer.

Hirschfeld's old friend—set designer Boris Aronson, who had been redefining what Broadway shows could look like since the 1930s—helped clarify what Sondheim needed to do. "I wrote the opening of *Company* as a matter of fact, after having seen a sketch by Boris Aronson. It showed me what I was writing for." Aronson evoked the bleak alienation of contemporary New Yorkers with a glass and chrome set of various levels, compartments, and two elevators.

For Hirschfeld, he found that all he needed to convey the characters' emotions was the performers themselves, eschewing any reference to Aronson's set. While there is no scene in the show where all the women piled on Bobby as seen in this drawing, it communicates exactly how the character felt being among them. Unconstrained by reality (although rooted in it), Hirschfeld captures the feeling of the show rather than simply a summation—he was a visual journalist who "reported" what he saw, looking for character, whether it was expressed in words, music, or movement, which he would then translate into his signature line. Hirschfeld summed up the equation as "My contribution is to take the character—created by the playwright and acted out by the actor—and reinvent it for the reader."

Sondheim bought this drawing from Hirschfeld and gave it to Hal Prince as a gift on opening night.

Company (revival)

TOP, FROM LEFT: Timothy Landfield, Patricia Ben Peterson and Danny Burstein; CENTER, FROM LEFT: Jane Krakowski, Debra Monk, Jonathan Dokuchitz, John Hilner, Veanne Cox, and Diana Canova; BOTTOM, FROM LEFT: Kate Burton, Boyd Gaines, La Chanze, Charlotte d'Amboise, and Robert Westenberg, 1995

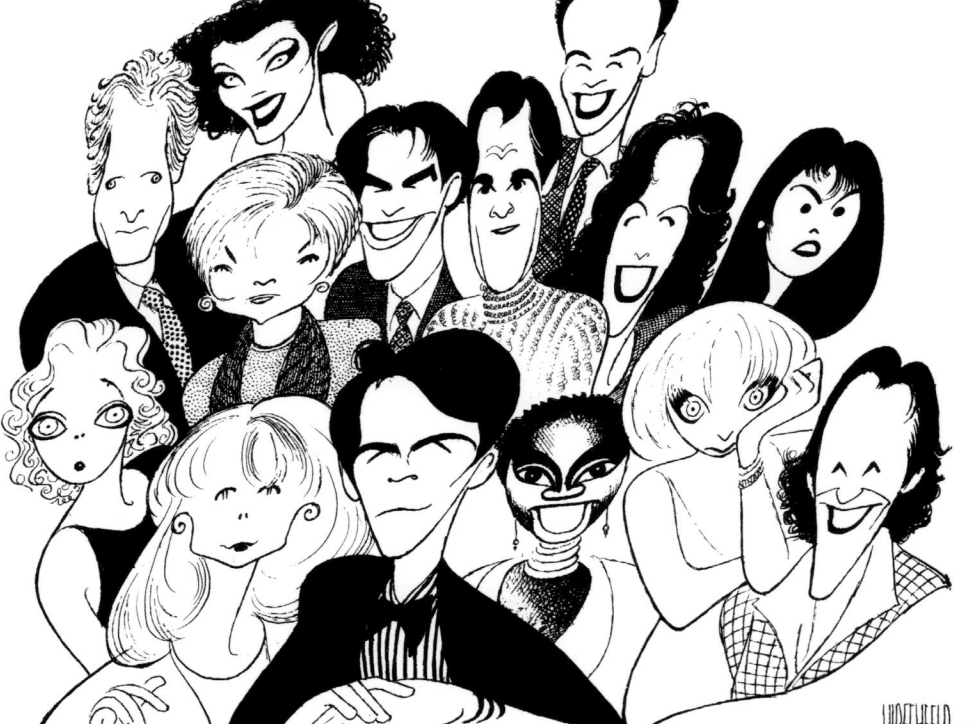

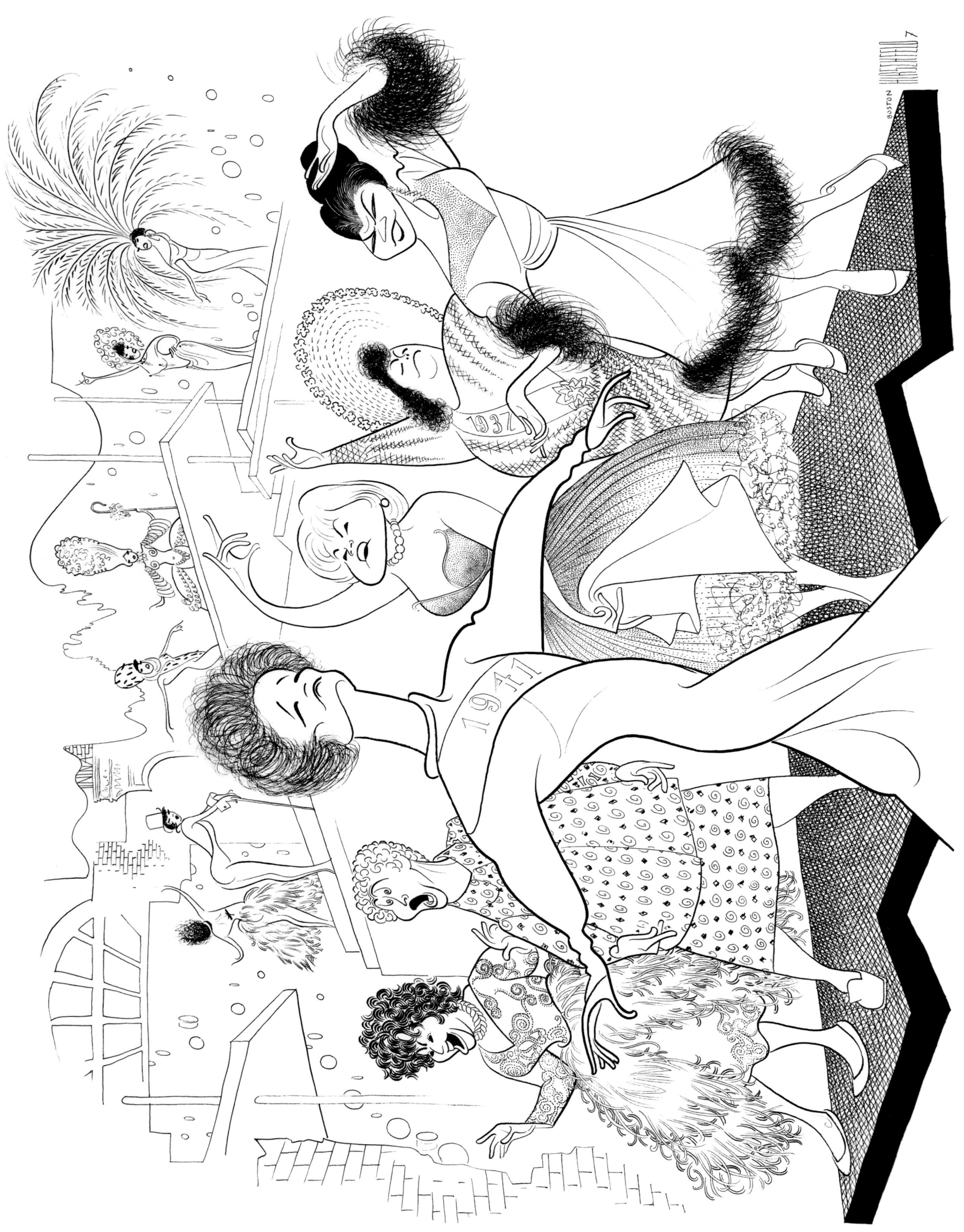

FOLLIES

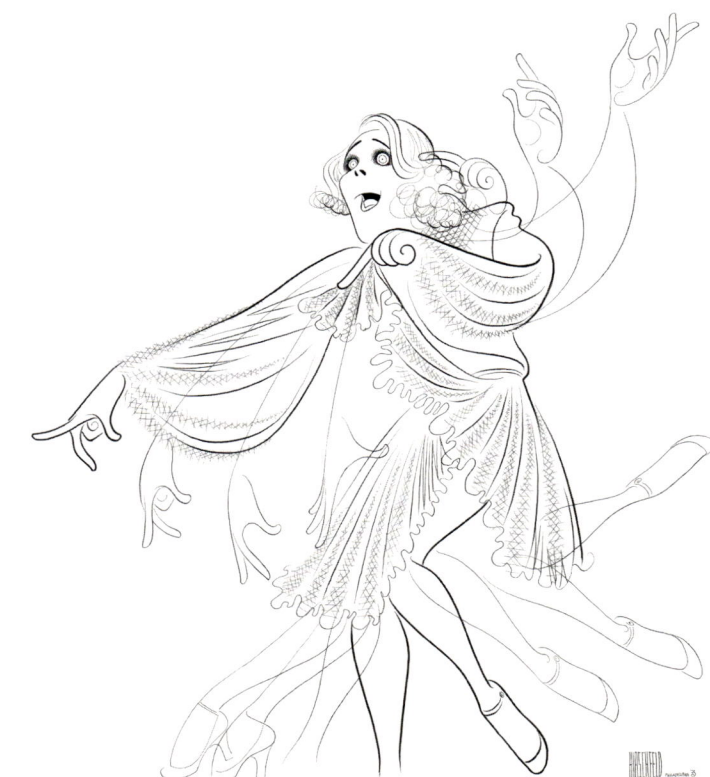

LEFT TO RIGHT: Fifi D'Orsay, Ethel Shutta, Alexis Smith,
Dorothy Collins, Mary McCarty, and Yvonne De Carlo

Ink on board, 1971

First published in the *New York Times*, April 4, 1971

Music and lyrics by Stephen Sondheim; book by James Goldman

OPENING DATE: April 4, 1971
CLOSING DATE: July 1, 1972
PERFORMANCES ON BROADWAY: 522

Nominated for eleven Tony Awards, it won seven:
- Best Original Score
- Best Direction of a Musical: Harold Prince and
  Michael Bennett
- Best Scenic Design: Boris Aronson
- Best Actress in a Musical: Alexis Smith
- Best Costume Design: Florence Klotz
- Best Lighting Design: Tharon Musser
- Best Choreography: Michael Bennett

Sondheim was creating a new type of musical, but he adored the
Broadway canon, even if he knew much of it only "through record-
ings and sheet music." Inspired by an article about a gathering of
former Ziegfeld Girls, in 1965 Sondheim asked playwright James
Goldman to write the book for a show about the reunion. While
the script went through many iterations, it turned into a plotless
musical about a reunion of performers from the fictional Weis-
mann Follies, focusing on the relationships between two cho-
rus girls from the 1941 edition and their husbands. The theme is
theater nostalgia, with the leads coming to terms with who they
are, while shadowed by ghosts of who they were.

Nostalgia was prevalent on Broadway at the time. With the
economy in recession, the war in Vietnam dragging on, and an
oil crisis that would soon produce staggering inflation, it may
be no surprise that audiences were happy with nostalgia and
mourned the passing of eras when life seemed less complicated.
Three months before *Follies*, a revival of the 1925 musical *No,
No Nanette* starring sixty-year-old dancer Ruby Keeler opened
and became one of the biggest hits of the season. Despite being
sixty-seven himself, Hirschfeld had little interest in looking
back. He lived in the present, as he had his whole life, which kept
him and his drawings eternally fresh, and welcomed the changes
Sondheim was making to the form.

Sondheim liked Hirschfeld's interpretation of the show so
much, he bought the original art for himself.

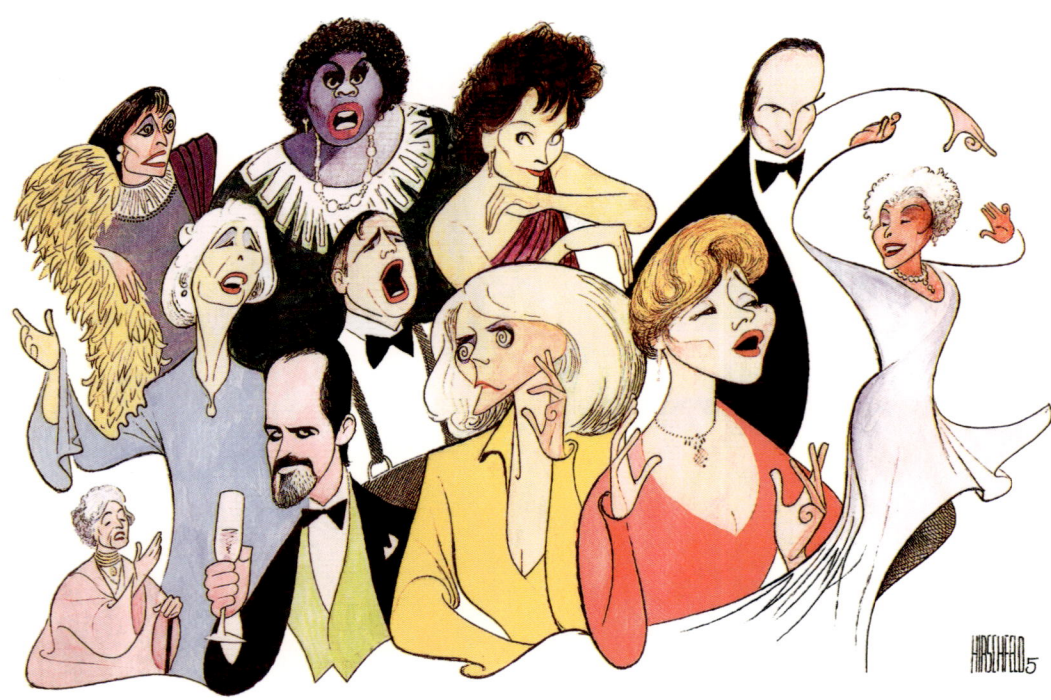

ABOVE
Ruby Keeler in *No, No Nanette*, 1971

LEFT
Follies (revival)

FOREGROUND (LEFT TO RIGHT):
Gregory Harrison, Blythe Danner,
and Judith Ivey; SECOND ROW: Joan
Roberts (seated), Betty Garrett,
Treat Williams, Polly Bergen, Donald
Saddler, and Marge Champion; REAR:
Jane White and Carol Woods, 2001

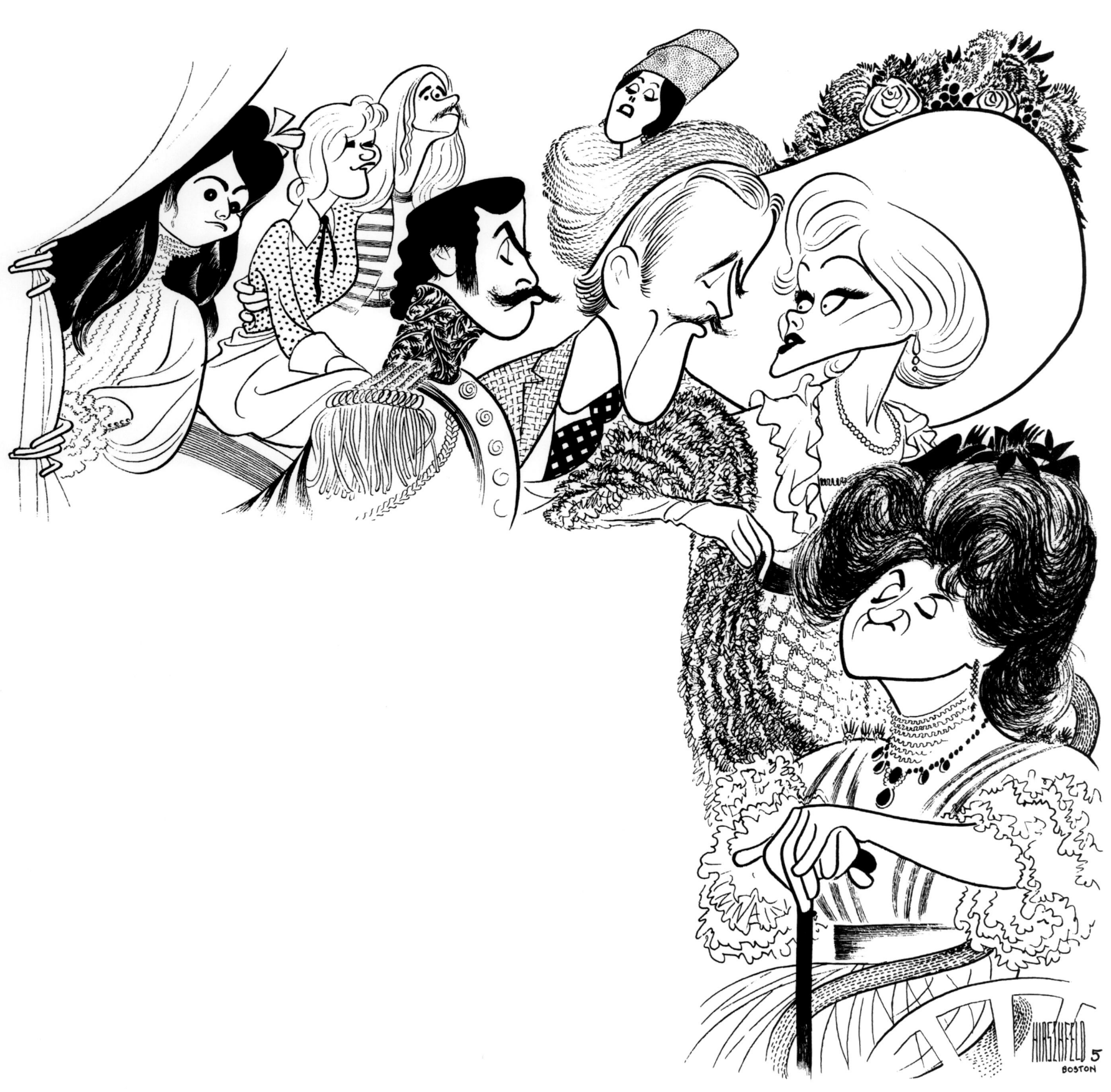

A LITTLE NIGHT MUSIC

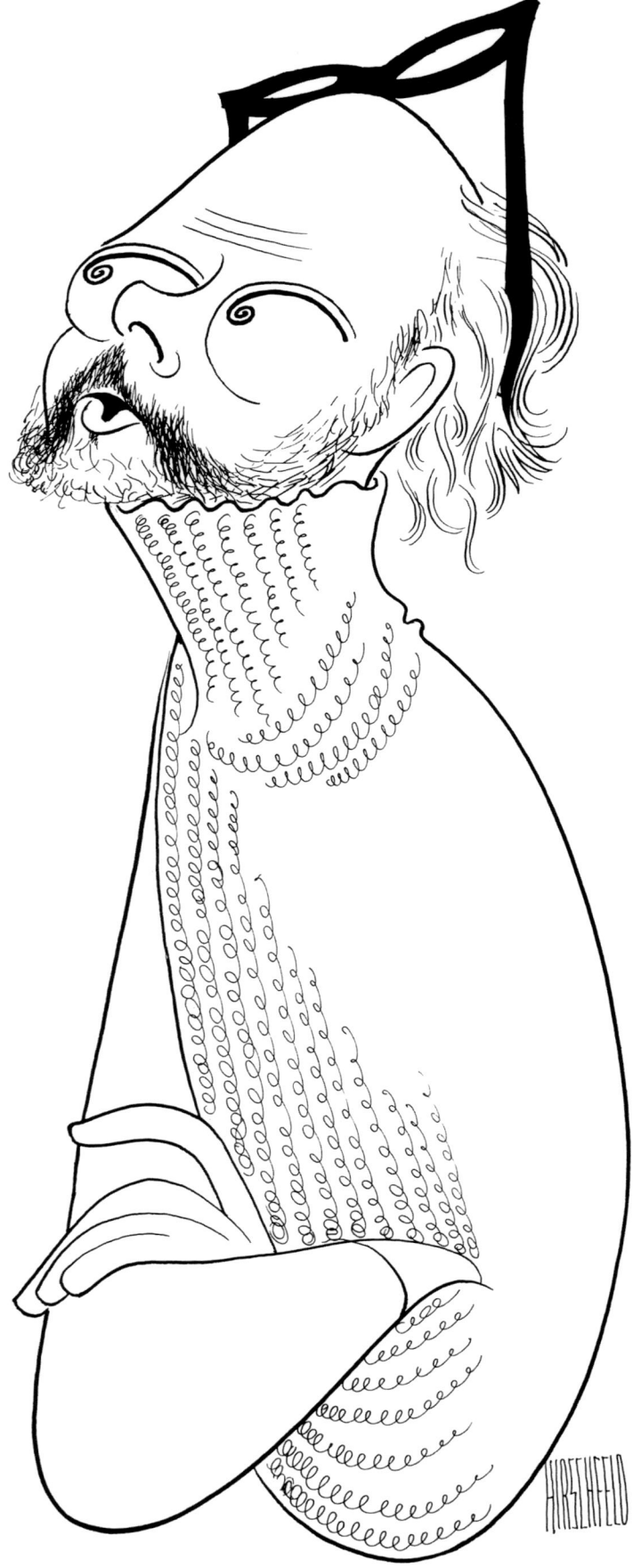

LEFT TO RIGHT: Victoria Mallory, Garn Stephens,
George Lee Andrews, Laurence Guittard, Patricia Elliott,
Len Cariou, Glynis Johns, and Hermione Gingold

Ink on board, 1973

First published in the *New York Times*, February 25, 1973

OPENING DATE: February 25, 1973
CLOSING DATE: August 3, 1974
PERFORMANCES ON BROADWAY: 601

Nominated for twelve Tony Awards, it won five:
○ Best Musical
○ Best Music and Lyrics: Stephen Sondheim
○ Best Book: Hugh Wheeler
○ Best Actress in a Musical: Glynis Johns
○ Best Supporting Actress in a Musical: Patricia Elliott

Sondheim's near operatic musical was inspired by the 1955 Ingmar Bergman film *Smiles of a Summer Night*, an evening of sexual musical chairs on the longest night of the year. The musical, a romantic farce about the lives of several upper-middle-class couples in early twentieth-century Sweden, includes one of Sondheim's best-known songs, "Send in the Clowns," written only days before the start of out-of-town tryouts.

Drawn by Hirschfeld during the tryout in Boston (as evidenced by the city's name next to Hirschfeld's signature), this artwork includes cast members who did not make it to New York, including Garn Stephens, who was replaced by D'Jamin-Bartlett as "Petra" the maid. This drawing was purchased by Sondheim from Hirschfeld. Sondheim had the cast, creative team, and producers sign the work and gave it to librettist Hugh Wheeler as an opening-night gift. The drawing was published the same day the show opened on Broadway.

The drawing's unusual shape was dictated by a request from the *Times*' art director, who was looking for fresh ways to present Hirschfeld's drawings in the Arts & Leisure section, which, for the previous four decades, had been primarily six-to-eight columns wide, at the top of the fold on the front page of the section. After some experimentation, the *Times* soon returned Hirschfeld to the top of page one of the section, where his work remained for the next thirty years until his last published piece, on December 15, 2002.

Hal Prince, producer and
director of *A Little Night Music*
Ink on board, 1978

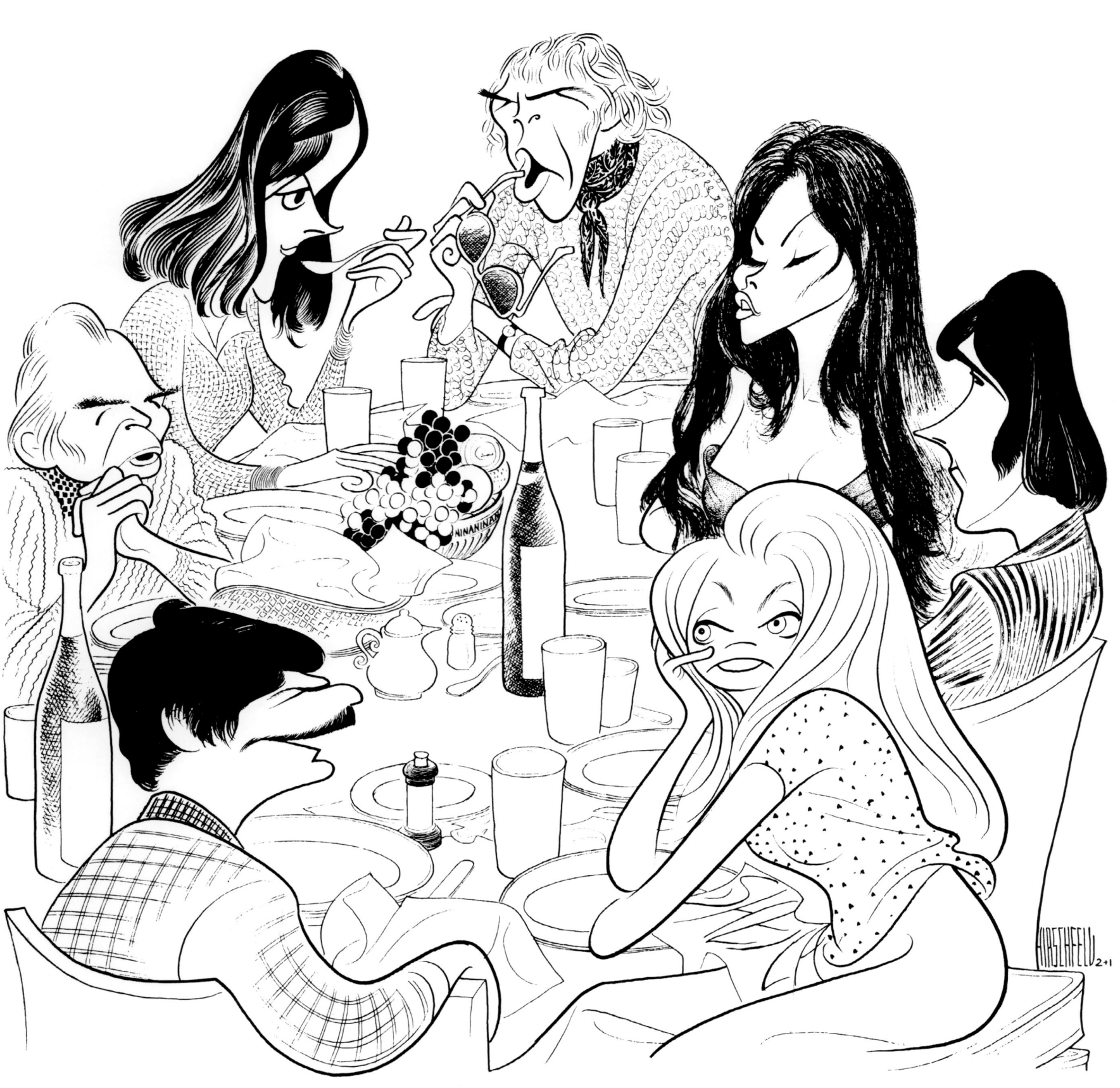

THE LAST OF SHEILA

CLOCKWISE FROM LEFT: James Mason, Joan Hackett, James Coburn, Raquel Welch, Ian McShane, Dyan Cannon, and Richard Benjamin

Ink on board, 1973

Publicity drawing to promote the Warner Bros. film; it appeared in publications all over the country.

Script by Stephen Sondheim and Anthony Perkins

Release date: June 14, 1973 (United States)

Sondheim loved games. He filled his houses with games and created scavenger hunts and mystery contests for his friends. He collaborated with actor Tony Perkins on some of them, and the two men shared a love of language, games, and murder mysteries. When director Herbert Ross asked Sondheim to write a murder mystery movie, Sondheim agreed only if he could work with Perkins. Their script involves a movie producer who gathers friends from a party a year earlier where his wife, Sheila, was killed in a hit-and-run—he believes by a party guest—so that he can use a series of elaborate games to find the killer.

Games were also a part of Hirschfeld's life. He began to hide his daughter's name—Nina—in the designs of his drawings when she was born in 1945. According to the artist, he put it "in folds of sleeves, tousled hairdos, eyebrows, wrinkles, backgrounds, shoelaces—anywhere to make it difficult, but not too difficult, to find." Over the next half century, Hirschfeld tried to end what he called "a national insanity," but he "learned, the hard way, to put Nina's name in the drawing before I proudly display my own signature."

Sunday mornings looking for NINAs was a custom shared by *New York Times* readers, a game played with children and grandchildren. Finding NINAs was an unspoken initiation into the worlds of Broadway, Off-Broadway, and Hollywood. For Hirschfeld, drawing NINAs became second nature, and they appeared spontaneously as he worked, forcing him to count them at the end like everyone else. At a reader's suggestion in 1960, he began to put a number next to his signature when there was more than one NINA to hunt for. For this drawing, he hid a SHEILA along with two NINAs.

Sondheim purchased this drawing from Hirschfeld and hung it in his New York City home.

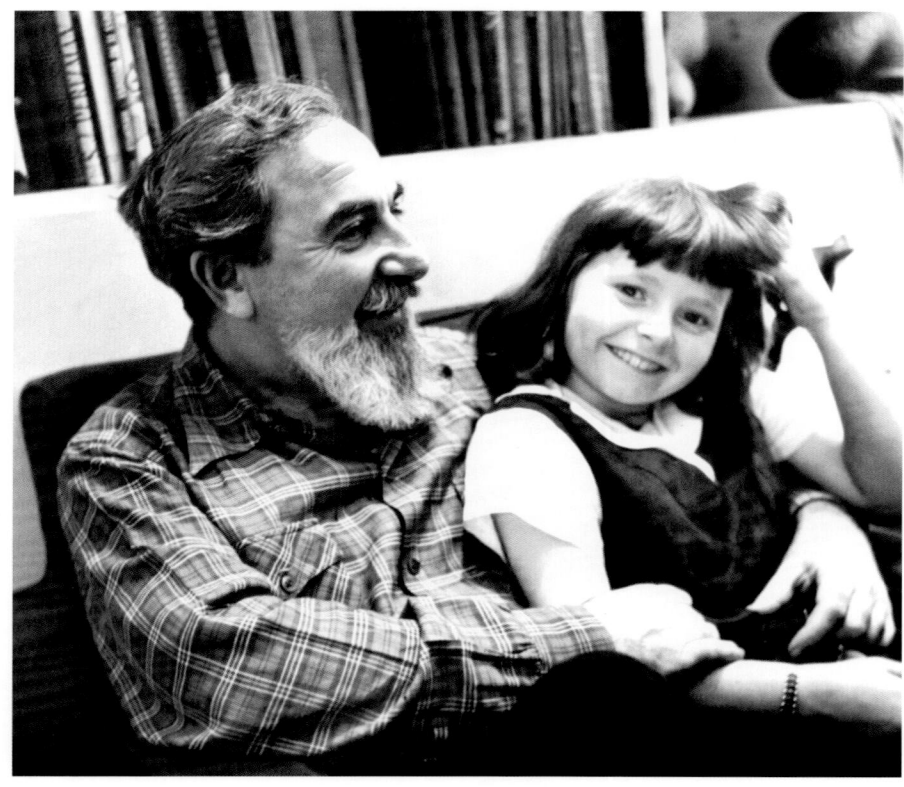

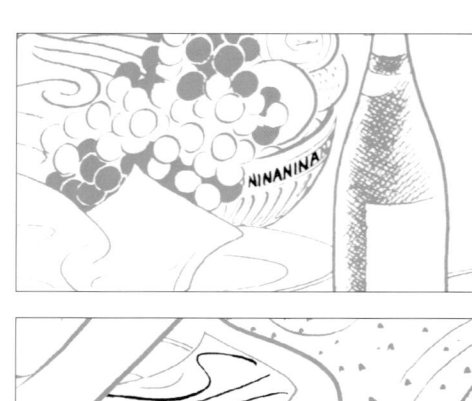

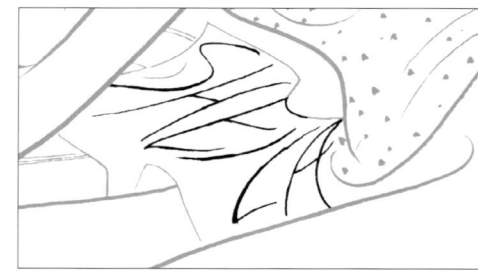

ABOVE
Details of *The Last of Sheila* drawing highlighting where the NINAs and SHEILA are hidden

LEFT
Hirschfeld at home with his daughter, Nina, c. 1954

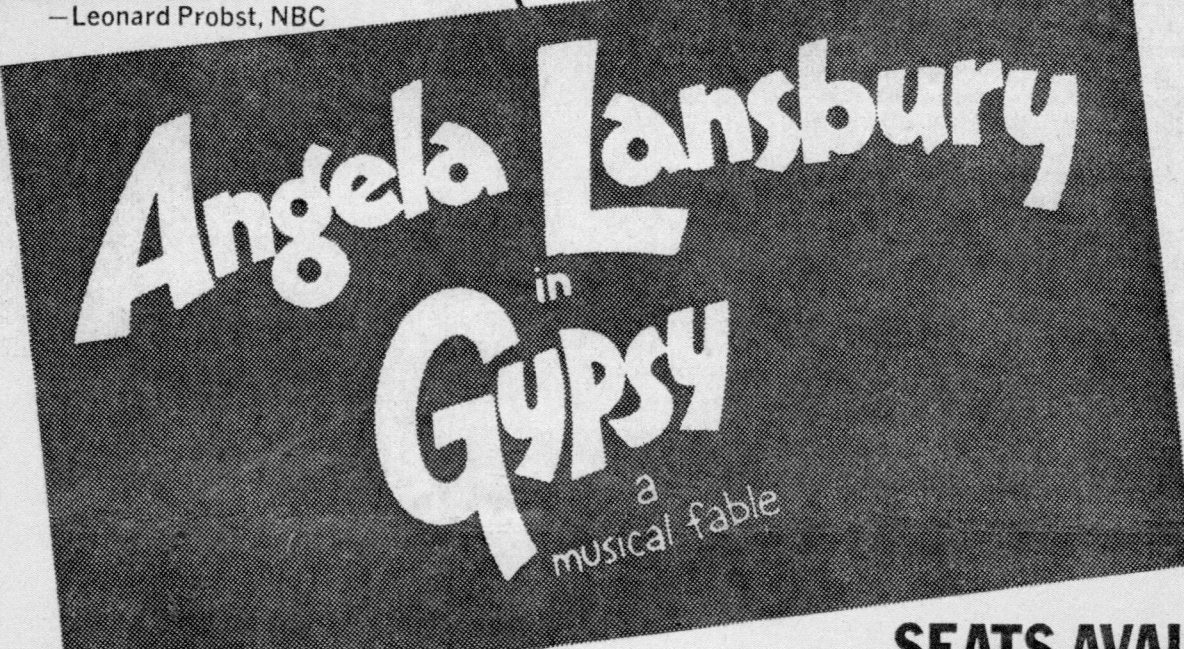

GYPSY

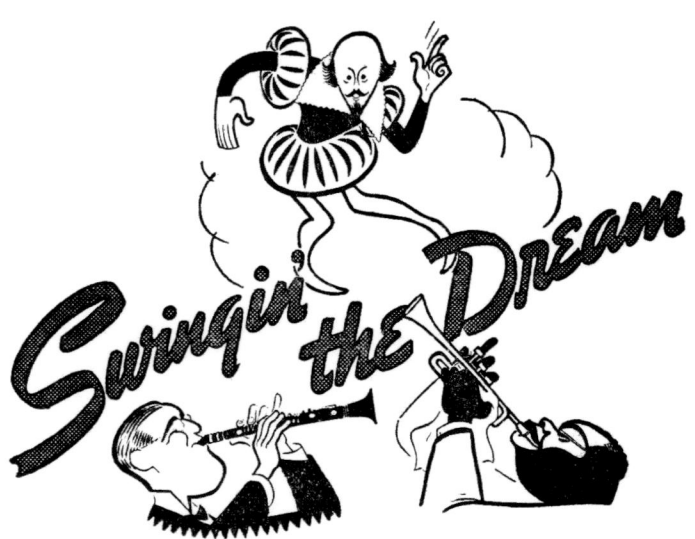

Angela Lansbury

Newspaper clipping, 1973

OPENING DATE: September 23, 1974
CLOSING DATE: January 4, 1975
PERFORMANCES ON BROADWAY: 120

Nominated for three Tony Awards, it won one:
○ Best Actress in a Musical: Angela Lansbury

Gypsy, the second Broadway show that Sondheim had written the lyrics for, was revived for the first time on Broadway fifteen years after it made its debut, with Angela Lansbury taking on the role of Mama Rose that Ethel Merman originated. The production began in the West End in 1973 and toured America for twenty-four weeks before coming to New York. Hirschfeld's drawing was used in print publicity throughout the tour and appeared in publications across the country.

While Hirschfeld had been drawing the theater for newspapers and magazines since 1926, he did not create his first show poster/logo until 1939—a jazz interpretation of Shakespeare's *A Midsummer Night's Dream* titled *Swingin' the Dream*. Over the next sixty years, Hirschfeld drew more theater posters than any other artist. His art was also used in theater print ads, programs, and cast albums.

ABOVE
Poster art for *Swingin' the Dream*, featuring Benny Goodman, William Shakespeare, and Louis Armstrong, 1939

BELOW
Gypsy
LEFT TO RIGHT: Jack Klugman, Ethel Merman, Sandra Church, Faith Dane, Maria Karnilova, and Chotzi Foley, 1959

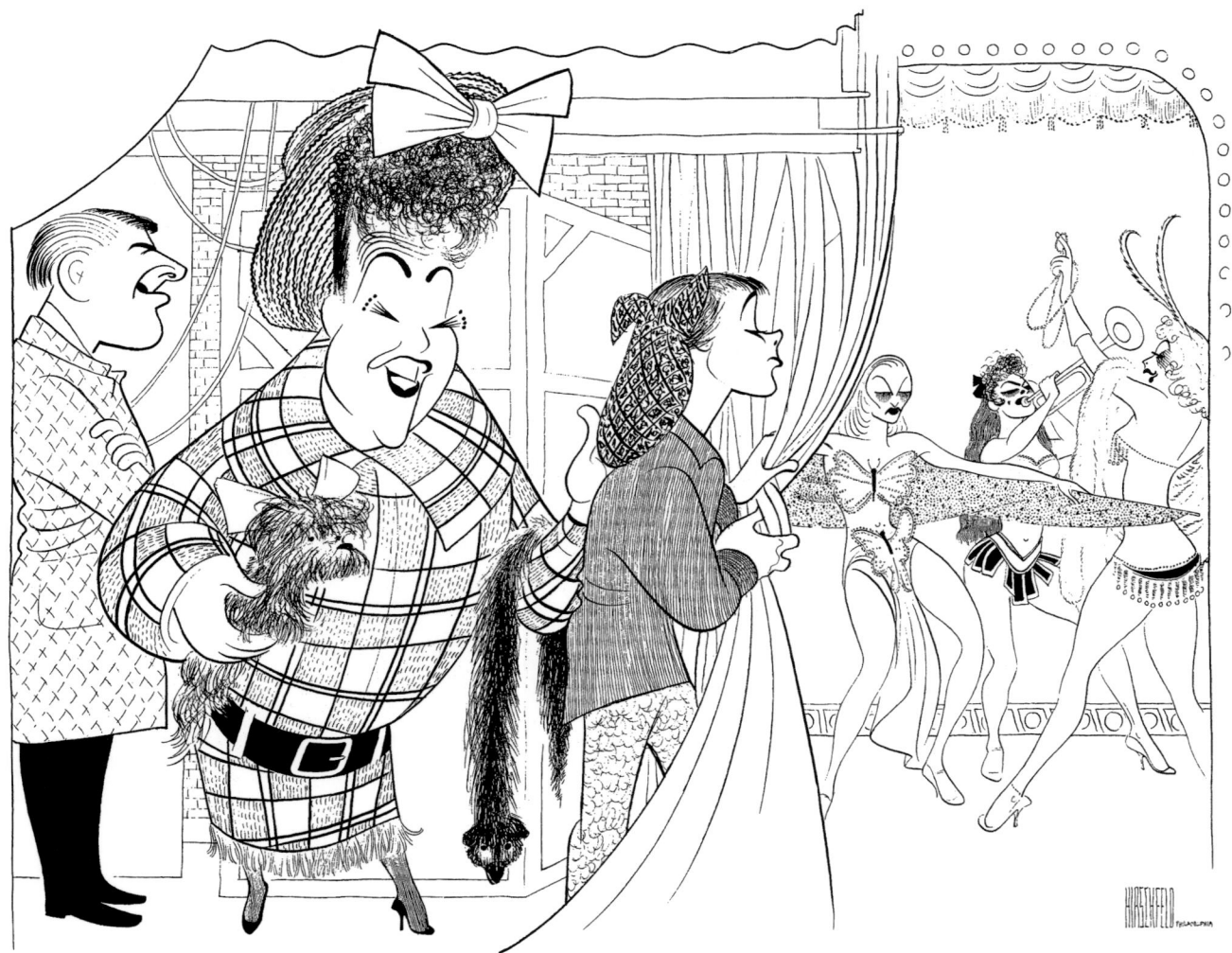

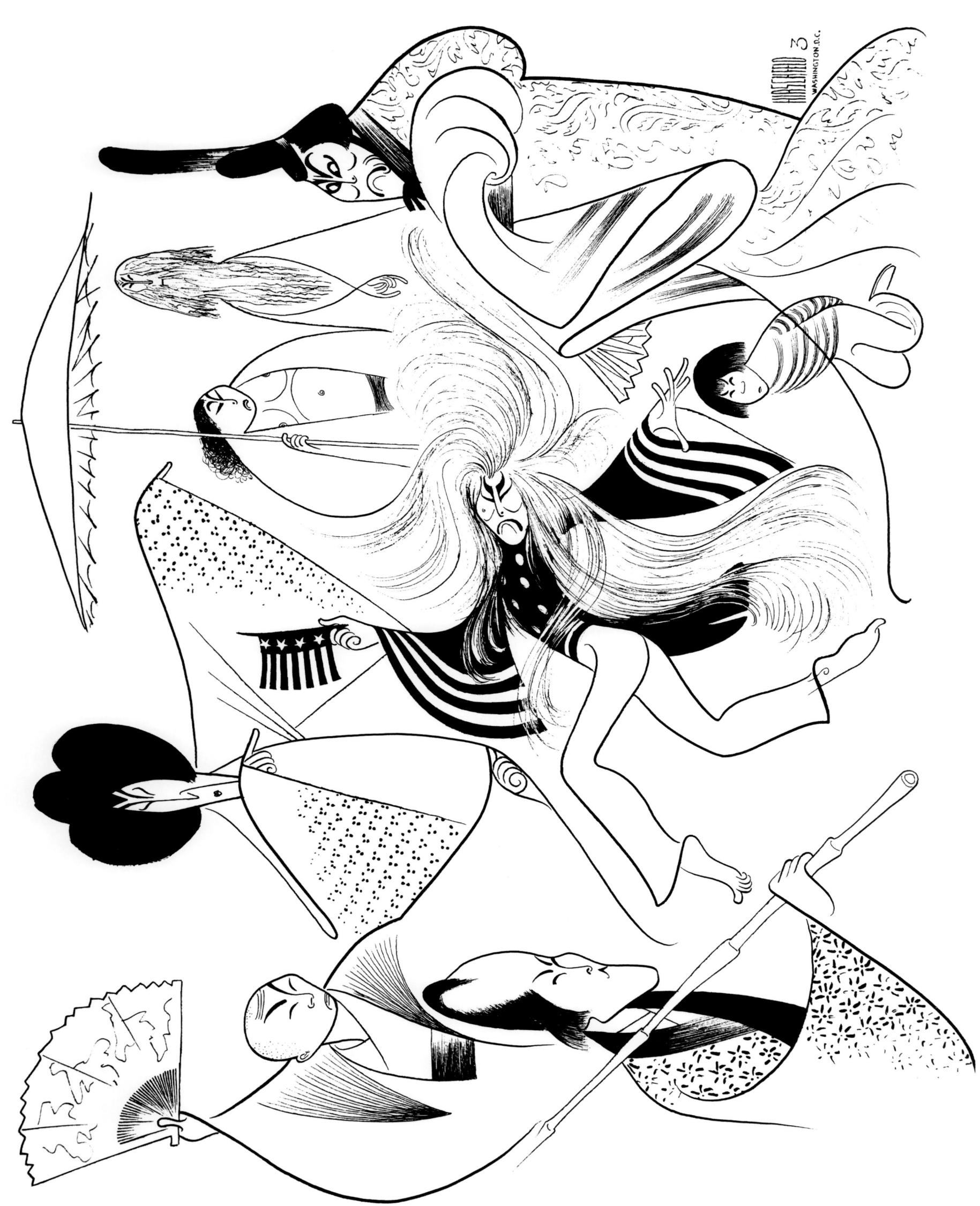

PACIFIC OVERTURES

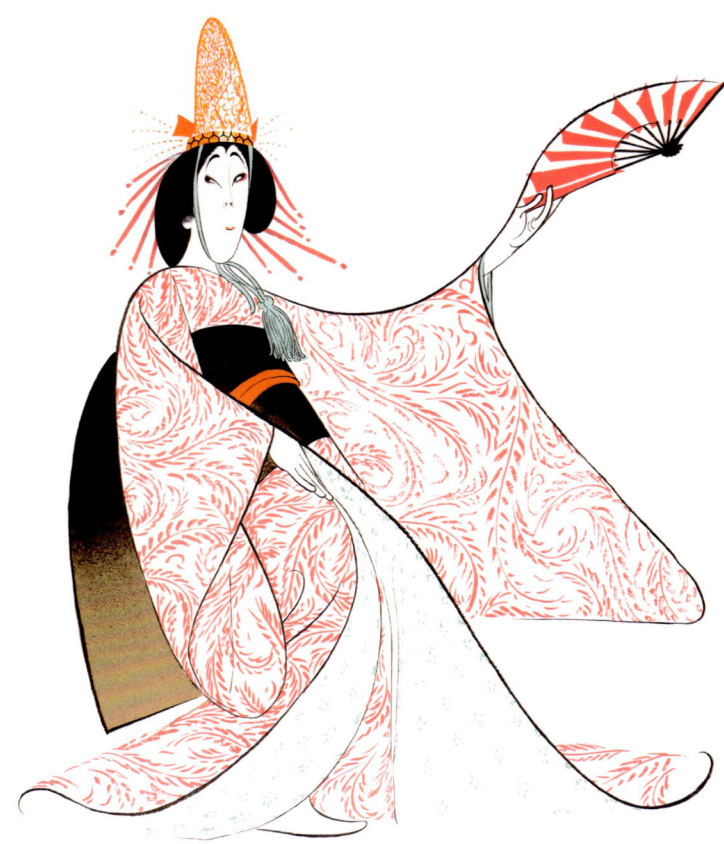

CLOCKWISE FROM BOTTOM LEFT: Isao Sato, Mako, Soon-Teck Oh, Conrad Yama, Freddy Mao, Yuki Shimoda, Sab Shimono, and (CENTER) Haruki Fujimoto

Ink on board, 1976

First published in the *New York Times*, January 18, 1976

Music and lyrics by Stephen Sondheim; book by John Weidman

OPENING DATE January 11, 1976
CLOSING DATE: June 27, 1976
PERFORMANCES ON BROADWAY: 193

Nominated for ten Tony Awards, it won two:
∘ Best Scenic Design: Boris Aronson
∘ Best Costume Design: Florence Klotz

At the start of his work on *Pacific Overtures*, Sondheim experienced an epiphany while looking at a threefold Japanese screen at the Metropolitan Museum of Art. Impressed by the simplicity of the design, he wrote, "The effect was magical—largely because, as with so much of Japanese art, what was omitted was as important as what was there." He had always been taught that "less is more," and while he understood it intellectually, he now felt it emotionally. He worked to make that leanness a style for his lyrics.

Hirschfeld experienced a similar epiphany a half century earlier when looking at Japanese drawings and woodcuts. His linear calligraphic style is a reaction to those works. He would later write, "I am much more influenced by the drawings of Harunobu, Utamaro, and Hokusai than I am by the painters of the West." Coincidentally, Hirschfeld visited Japan just before *Pacific Overtures* opened, and he returned home to create a series of drawings, paintings, and prints of the Kabuki theater (which also inspired the costumes in the musical). With the performers in Sondheim's show costumed like Kabuki performers, Hirschfeld must have been delighted to bring these two passions together.

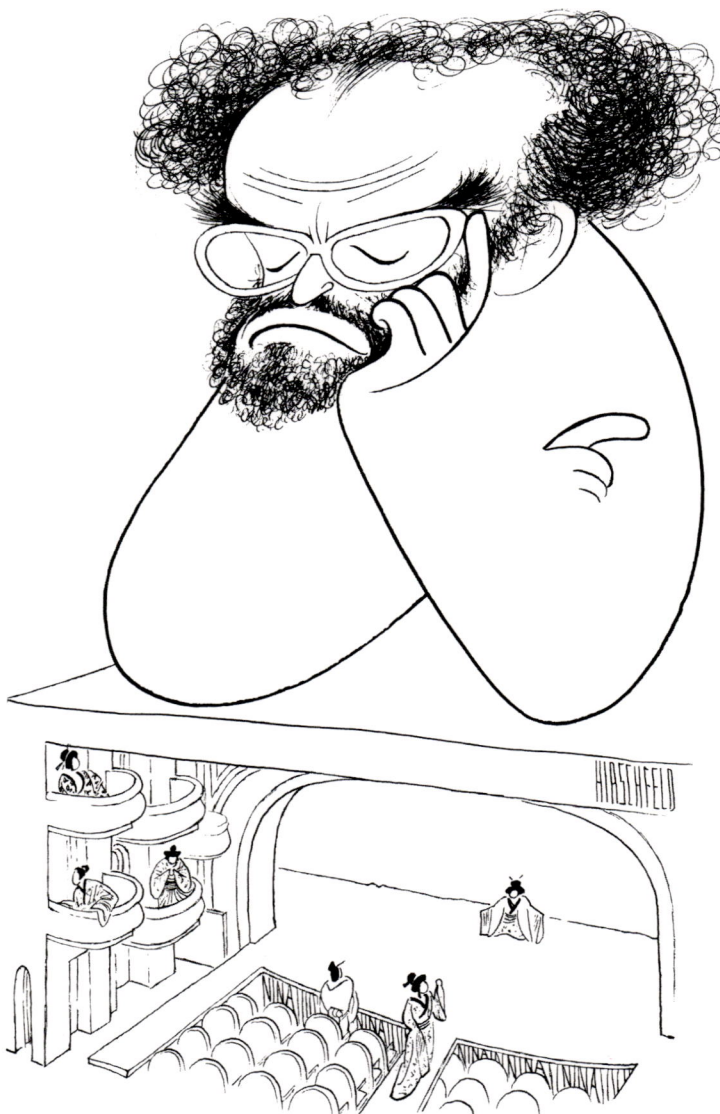

TOP
Kanonko from the Kabuki series
Lithograph on paper, 1976

RIGHT
Boris Aronson, 1976

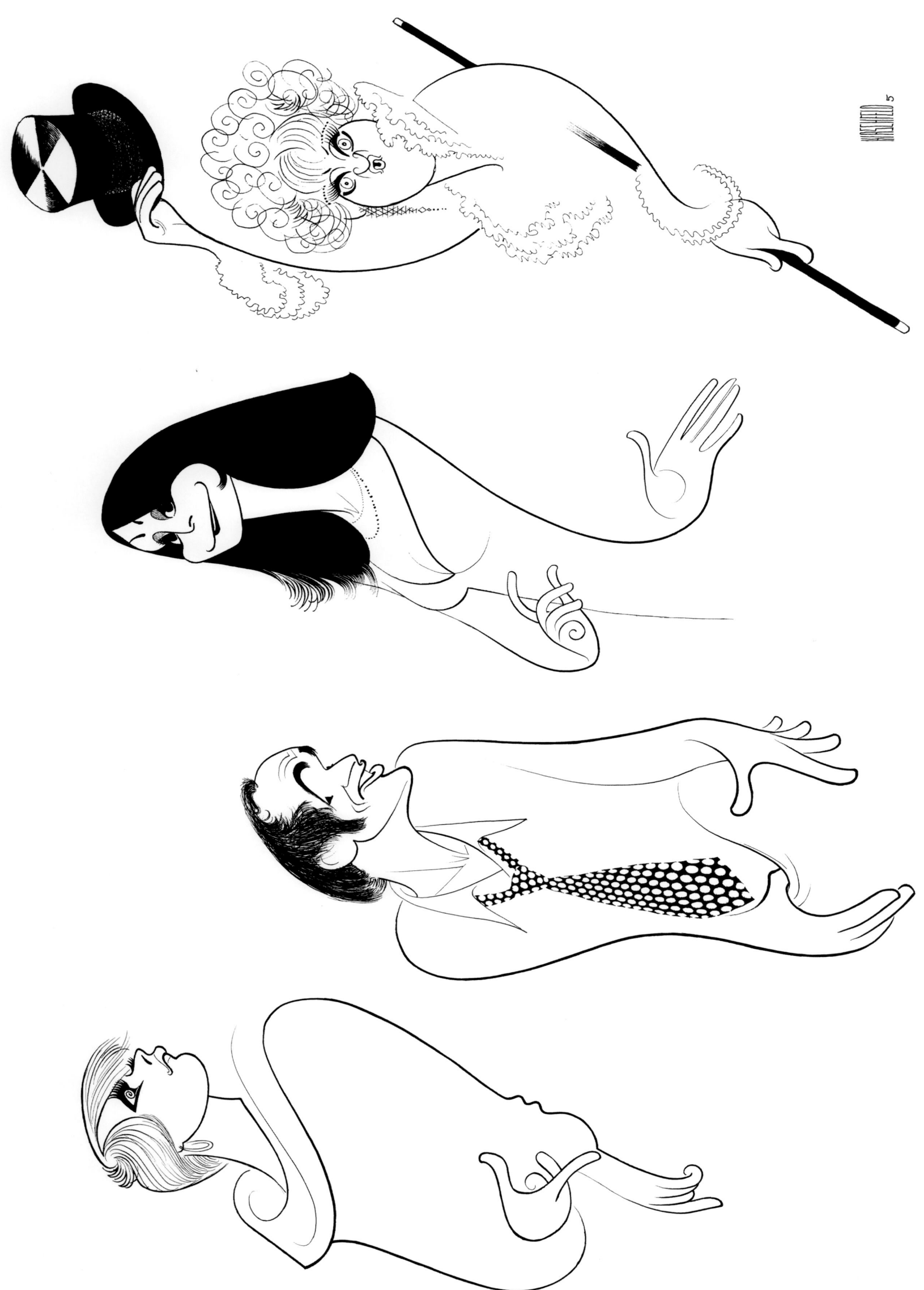

SIDE BY SIDE BY SONDHEIM

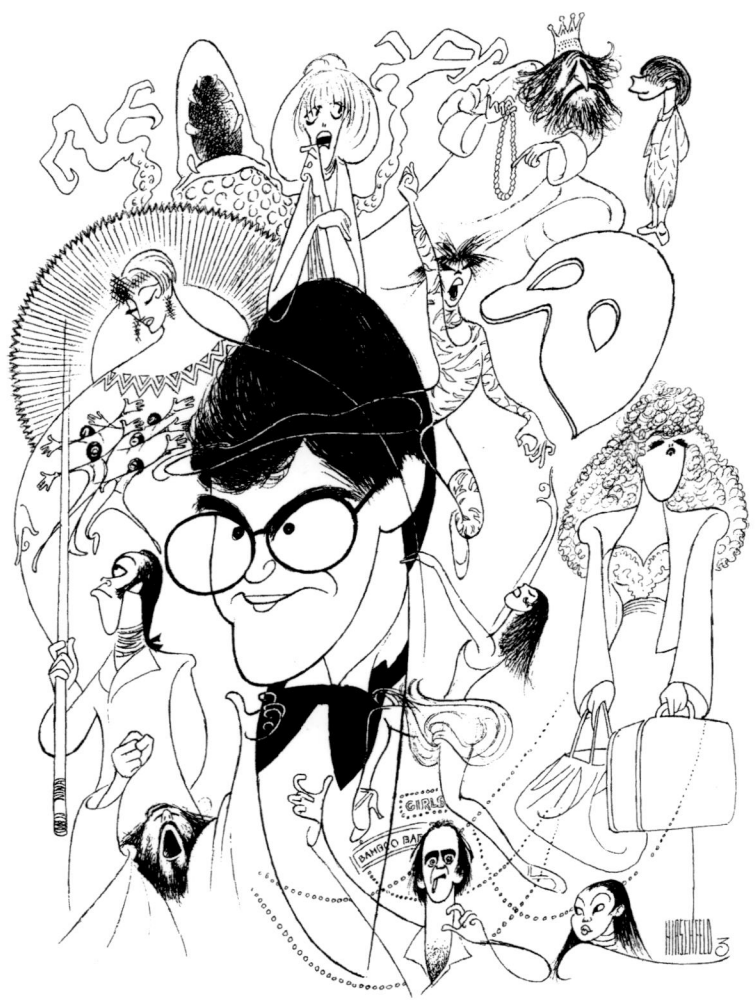

Nancy Dussault

First published in the *New York Times*, September 2, 1977

Larry Kert

First published in the *New York Times*, July 29, 1977

Georgia Brown

First published in the *New York Times*, November 11, 1977

Hermione Gingold

First published in the *New York Times*, December 9, 1977

Ink on board, 1977

Music and lyrics by Stephen Sondheim; additional music by Leonard Bernstein, Mary Rodgers, Richard Rodgers, and Jule Styne; continuity by Ned Sherrin

OPENING DATE: April 18, 1977
CLOSING DATE: March 19, 1978
PERFORMANCES ON BROADWAY: 384

Nominated for five Tony Awards, including Best Musical

When David Kernan was playing in the original West End production of *A Little Night Music*, he was asked to put together a revue for a small theater outside of London. Kernan and director

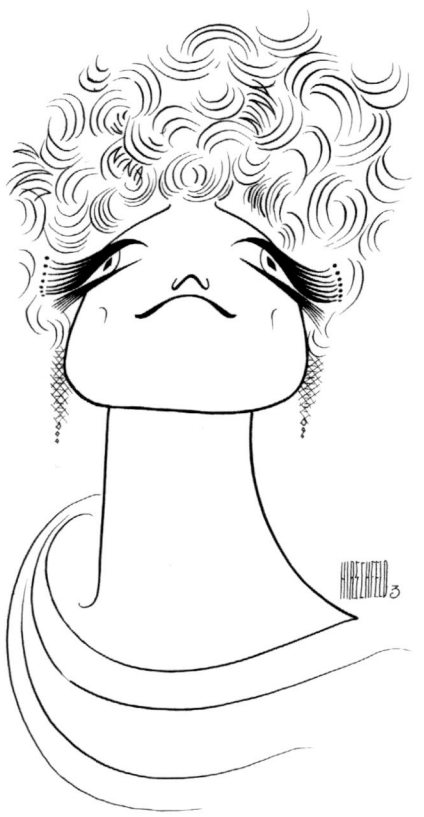

ABOVE
Cameron Mackintosh, surrounded by shows he produced, 1992

LEFT
Julia McKenzie in *Side by Side by Sondheim*, 1976

Ned Sherrin decided on a revue of Sondheim material. When they wrote to him for permission, Sondheim sent a telegram: "By all means try, but I can't think of anything more boring except possibly the *Book of Kells*." Cameron Mackintosh, just starting out as a producer, transferred the revue to London, where it ran for three years. Hal Prince agreed to produce a Broadway version, and persuaded Actors' Equity to allow the original British cast to transfer with the show. After Tony nominations for the show and all four actors, the British cast was incrementally replaced by Nancy Dussault, Larry Kert, Georgia Brown, and Hermione Gingold as the Narrator. Hirschfeld drew the full American cast, individually, and the drawings appeared over six months in the Friday theater column of the *Times*.

The Friday column started only a year earlier, and naturally the *Times* asked Hirschfeld to contribute. The space where his drawings would be seen, on the second page of the Weekend section, was never more than six by three inches, and occasionally even smaller. For a man working on a board that was roughly twenty by thirty inches, and who always preached that one should know their limitations, the confines of the single-column space provided a regular testing ground for distilling his line even further. These weekly works were the laboratory for Hirschfeld to explore what he could do with line. Focusing on one performer in a single show, and for a very small space, pushed him to refine his work even more. Week in and week out, he was continually exploring what he could draw and/or not draw to make an effective work.

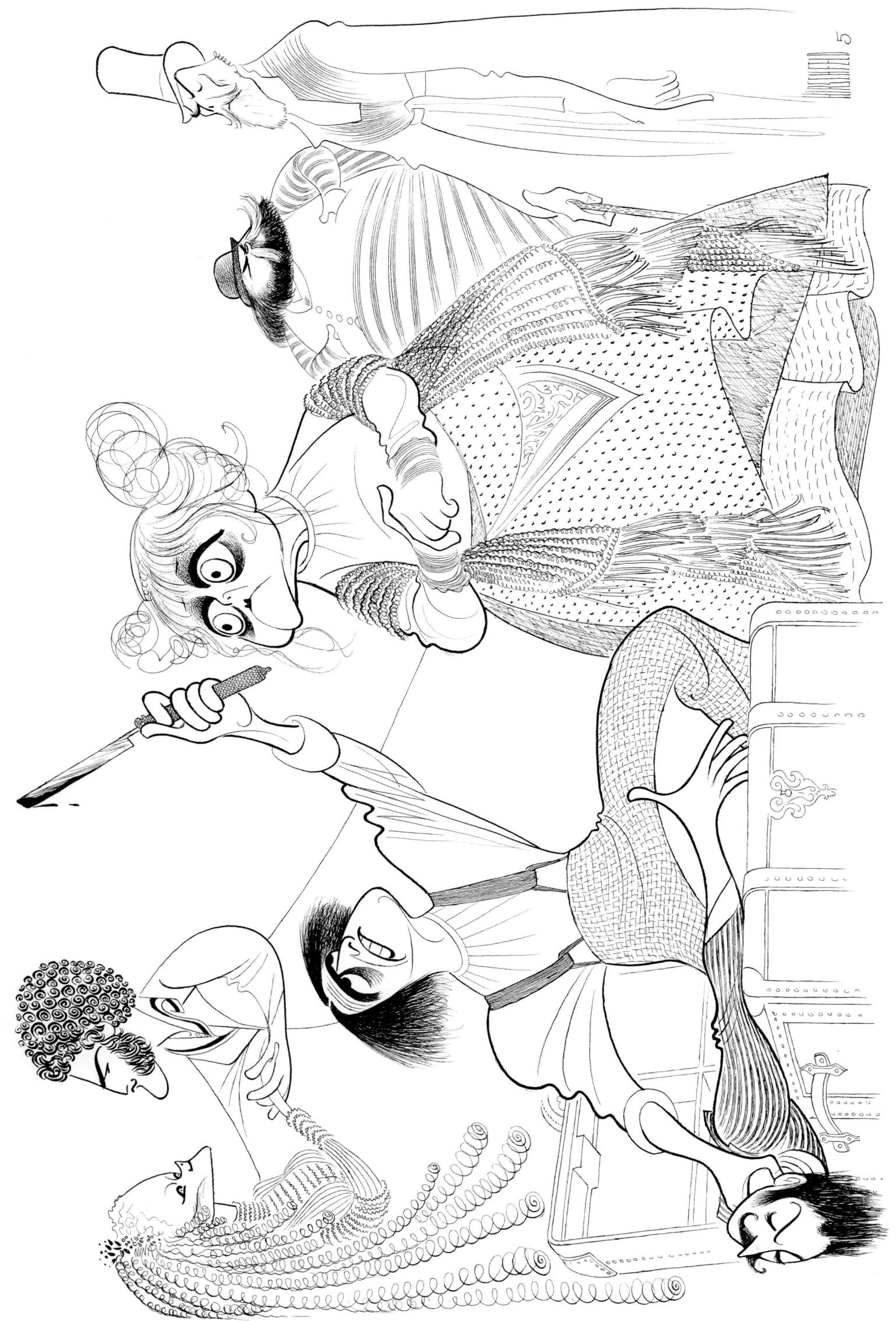

SWEENEY TODD: THE DEMON BARBER OF FLEET STREET

LEFT TO RIGHT: Sarah Rice, Victor Garber,
Joaquin Romaguera, Len Cariou, Angela Lansbury,
Jack Eric Williams, and Edmund Lyndeck

Ink on board, 1979

First published in the *New York Times*, February 25, 1979

Music and lyrics by Stephen Sondheim; book by
Hugh Wheeler, based on the play *Sweeney Todd:
The Demon Barber of Fleet Street* by Christopher Bond

OPENING DATE: March 1, 1979
CLOSING DATE: June 29, 1980
PERFORMANCES ON BROADWAY: 557

Nominated for nine Tony Awards, it won eight:
○ Best Musical
○ Best Original Score
○ Best Book of a Musical
○ Best Direction of a Musical: Harold Prince
○ Best Actor in a Musical: Len Cariou
○ Best Actress in a Musical: Angela Lansbury
○ Best Scenic Design: Eugene Lee
○ Best Costume Design: Franne Lee

Sweeney Todd (revival)

LEFT TO RIGHT: Jim Walton, Gretchen Kingsley, Michael McCarty, Bill
Nabel, Bob Gunton, David Barron, Beth Fowler, and Eddie Korbich, 1989

When Sondheim was in London for the opening of a revival of *Gypsy* with Angela Lansbury, he saw Christopher Bond's play and was enchanted by how Bond had changed "a dreadful Victorian relic" into a "first rate play." While the songs came to him quickly, the show's major theme came slowly to Sondheim. "I never start with subject matter . . . I always discover the subject I'm writing about as I write." Only when Harold Prince's wife, Judy, heard the songs for the first time did he realize, after she pointed it out, that the songs were the story of his life. The "musical thriller" would go on to be one of Sondheim's most popular shows.

When Hirschfeld went to see an early preview, he had no idea what he would encounter, and that did not disturb him at all. He was looking for the gesture, expression, and/or movement that would reveal the character onstage and of the show itself. Hirschfeld taught himself to draw in the dark, as there was little ambient light in a dark theater to see his sketchpad, and he did not want to disturb others in the audience. He kept a small pad in his pocket, and he made sketches without looking. He once described it as "a collaboration of sight and hand, with no conscious thought at the controls." When he returned to his studio, he would review his sketches and often look at press photos (to ensure accuracy). Just as Sondheim discovered his subjects as he wrote, Hirschfeld discovered what his drawings would look like as he drew them.

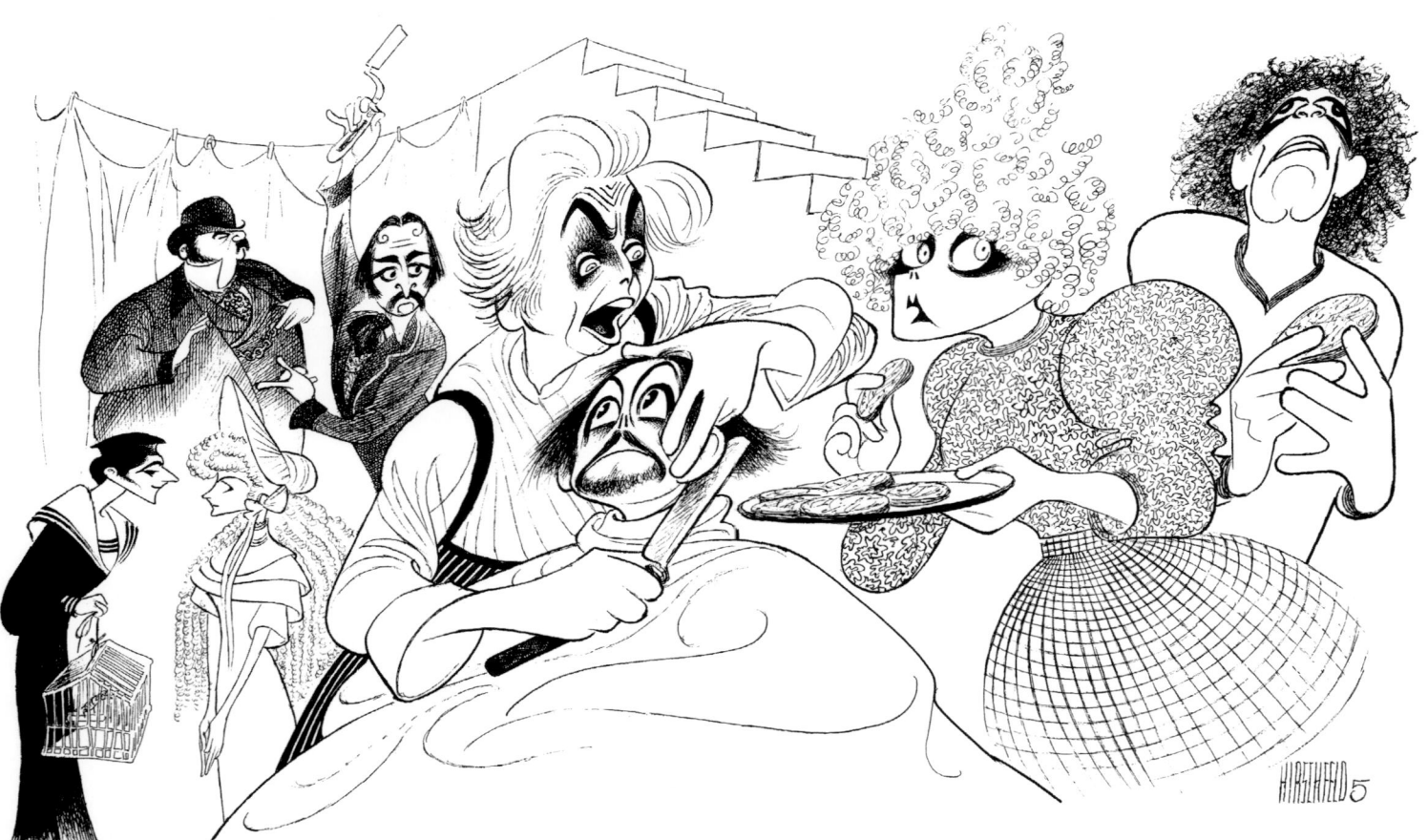

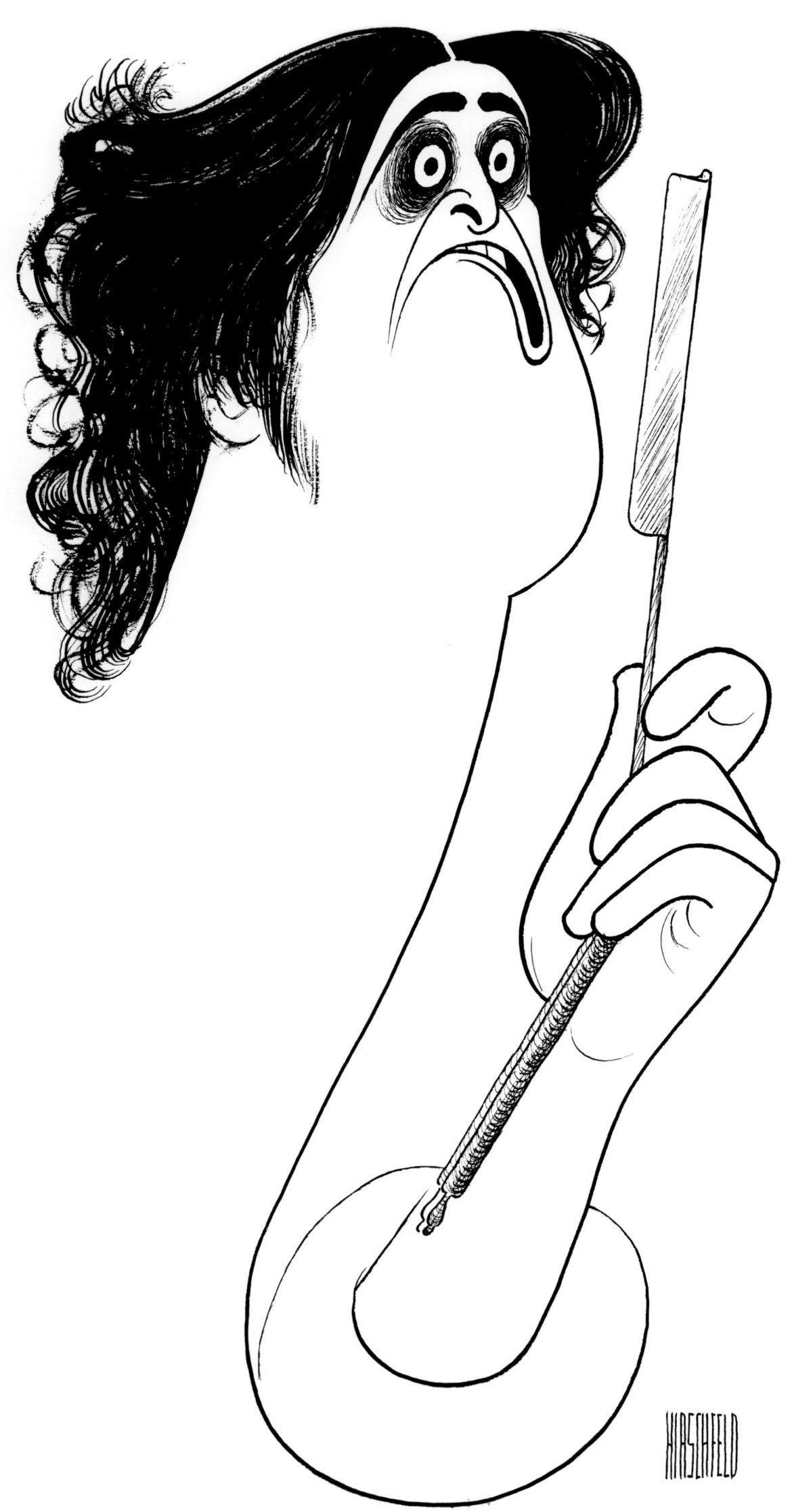

LEN CARIOU in SWEENEY TODD: THE DEMON BARBER OF FLEET STREET

Ink on board, 1979

First published in the *New York Times*, April 20, 1979

Music and lyrics by Stephen Sondheim; book by
Hugh Wheeler, based on the play *Sweeney Todd:
The Demon Barber of Fleet Street* by Christopher Bond

OPENING DATE: March 1, 1979
CLOSING DATE: June 29, 1980
PERFORMANCES ON BROADWAY: 557

Winner of the Tony Award for Best Actor in a Musical: Len Cariou

In the summer of 1976, Sondheim and Hal Prince approached Len Cariou about playing the lead in *Sweeney Todd*. Cariou was acting in the film adaptation of *A Little Night Music*, and the project kept getting postponed. But once it did open, Cariou was quoted in the *Times* Friday theater column this drawing appeared in, saying that his Shakespeare experience had helped him. "The essence of Sondheim is to make his intent clear. There's a corollary in singing, all in one breath, 'There's a hole in the world like a great black pit . . .' and in doing, oh, Lear's speech to his daughters. You try to do that all in one breath, and you try to get the sense of it and the intent, just as in Sondheim."

The Friday drawings were a diary not only of what Hirschfeld saw, but also of what interested him graphically. There has never been such a diary of an artist's work of his stature that played out in public every week. To look at the Friday drawings now is to realize that this is where Hirschfeld was experimenting with his art the most during this period. In 1983, he was quoted as saying, "I want to keep simplifying my graphic description of someone's character. Now I am down to a pencil, a pen, and bottle of ink. I hope one day to eliminate the pencil." Hirschfeld's Friday drawings reveal how close he was to achieving this aim.

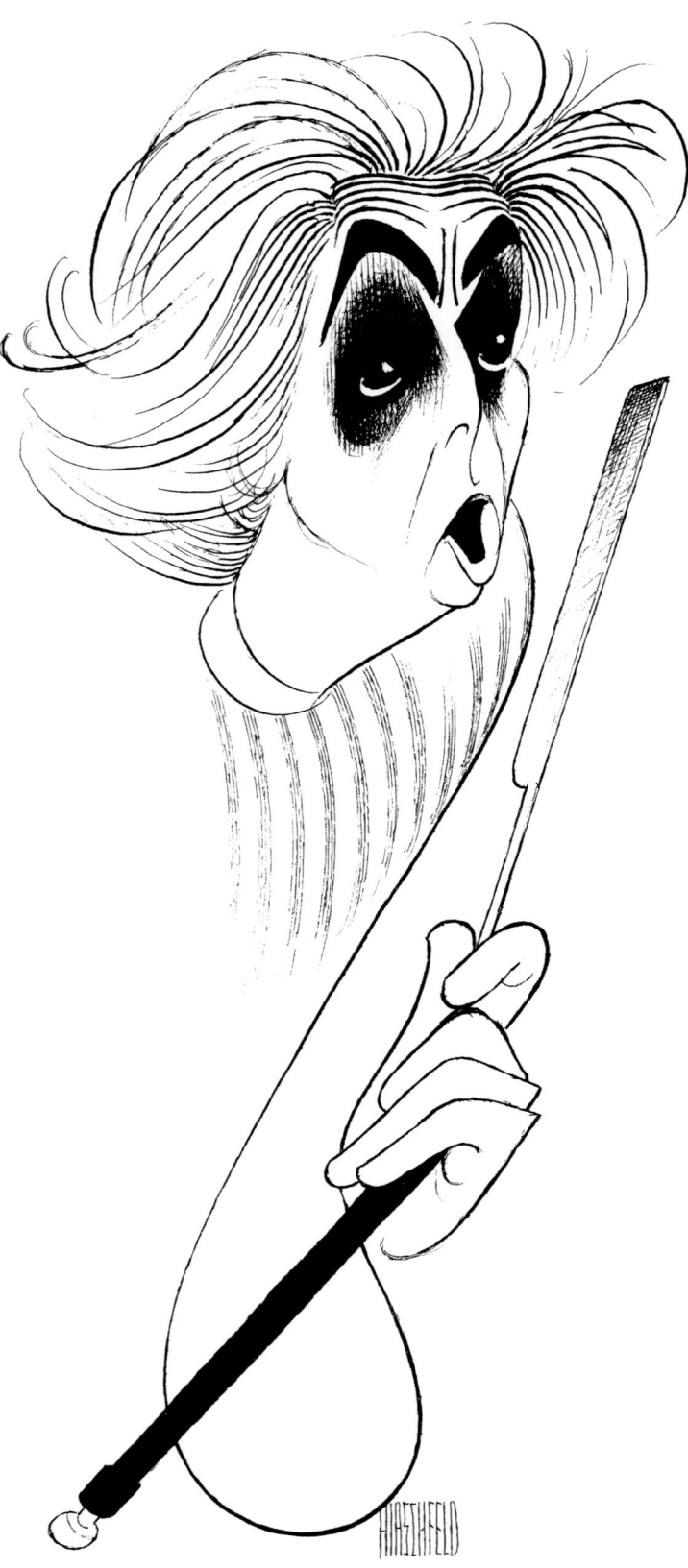

Bob Gunton in the revival of *Sweeney Todd:
The Demon Barber of Fleet Street*, 1989

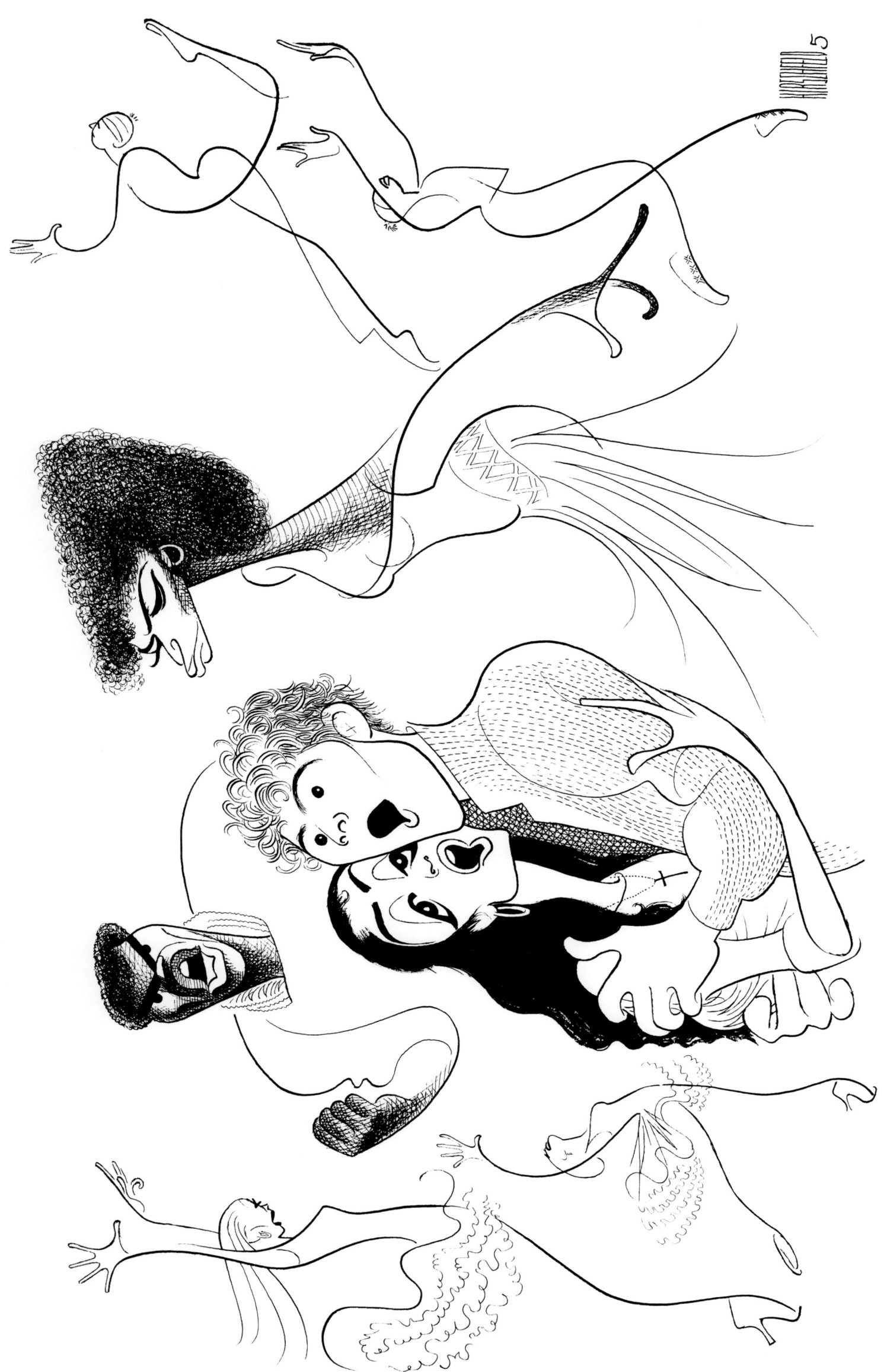

WEST SIDE STORY (revival)

LEFT TO RIGHT: Hector Jaime Mercado, Josie de Guzman, Ken Marshall, and Debbie Allen

Ink on board, 1980

First published in the *New York Times*, February 7, 1980

Lyrics by Stephen Sondheim; music by Leonard Bernstein; book by Arthur Laurents; conceived, directed, and choreographed by Jerome Robbins

OPENING DATE: February 14, 1980
CLOSING DATE: November 30, 1980
PERFORMANCES ON BROADWAY: 333

Nominated for three Tony Awards, including Best Revival

Hirschfeld, in his barber chair at the drawing table, 1986. Both chair and table are now on view at the entrance of the New York Public Library for the Performing Arts at Lincoln Center.

After the success of *Fiddler on the Roof* in 1964, which Jerry Robbins both directed and choreographed, Robbins left Broadway for sixteen years to return to the world of ballet before directing and choreographing this revival of *West Side Story*. Although most of the cast had not been born when the original production debuted in 1957, Robbins felt little need to update the work. "It is a period piece. We might have made many changes, but the show is a product of its time. We've reached a point now where revivals are not merely substitutes for new shows but can be seen as legitimate repertory."

The only other show that Robbins would direct on Broadway was *Jerome Robbins' Broadway*, a 1989 revue of Robbins choreography that surveyed his whole career. Robbins had a remarkable twenty-year run as a director and/or choreographer. He started even earlier as a performer, in 1938. He was like a comet that blazed brightly for two decades, illuminating the way for many others to follow his path, but then was gone. Hirschfeld had been capturing Broadway for a dozen years before Robbins made his first appearance on the Great White Way, and would continue for more than dozen years after Robbins took his victory lap in 1989. The world of Broadway was always changing, yet one thing that seemed constant was Al Hirschfeld, whose work seemed more and more like an eternal flame rather than a comet.

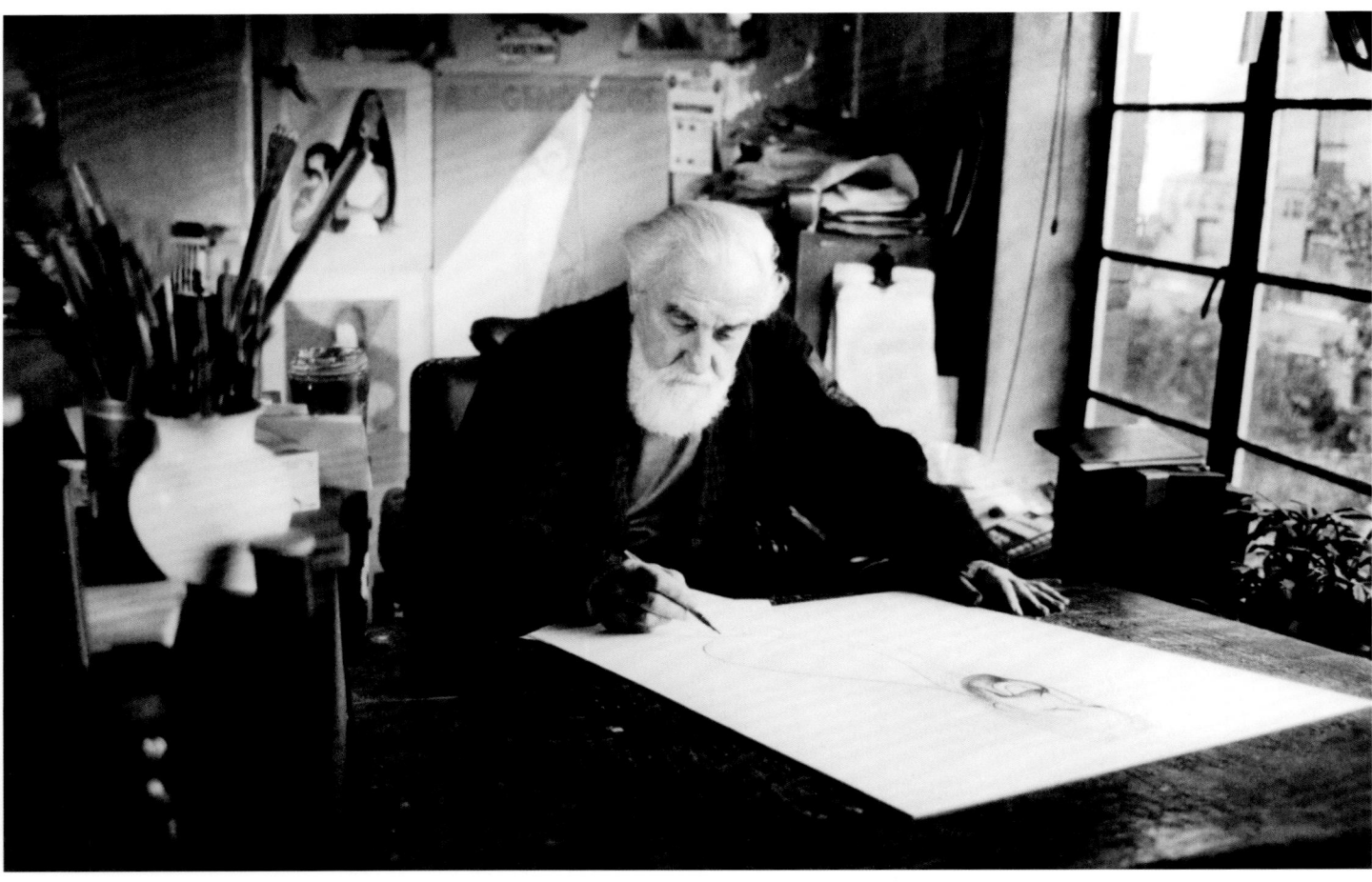

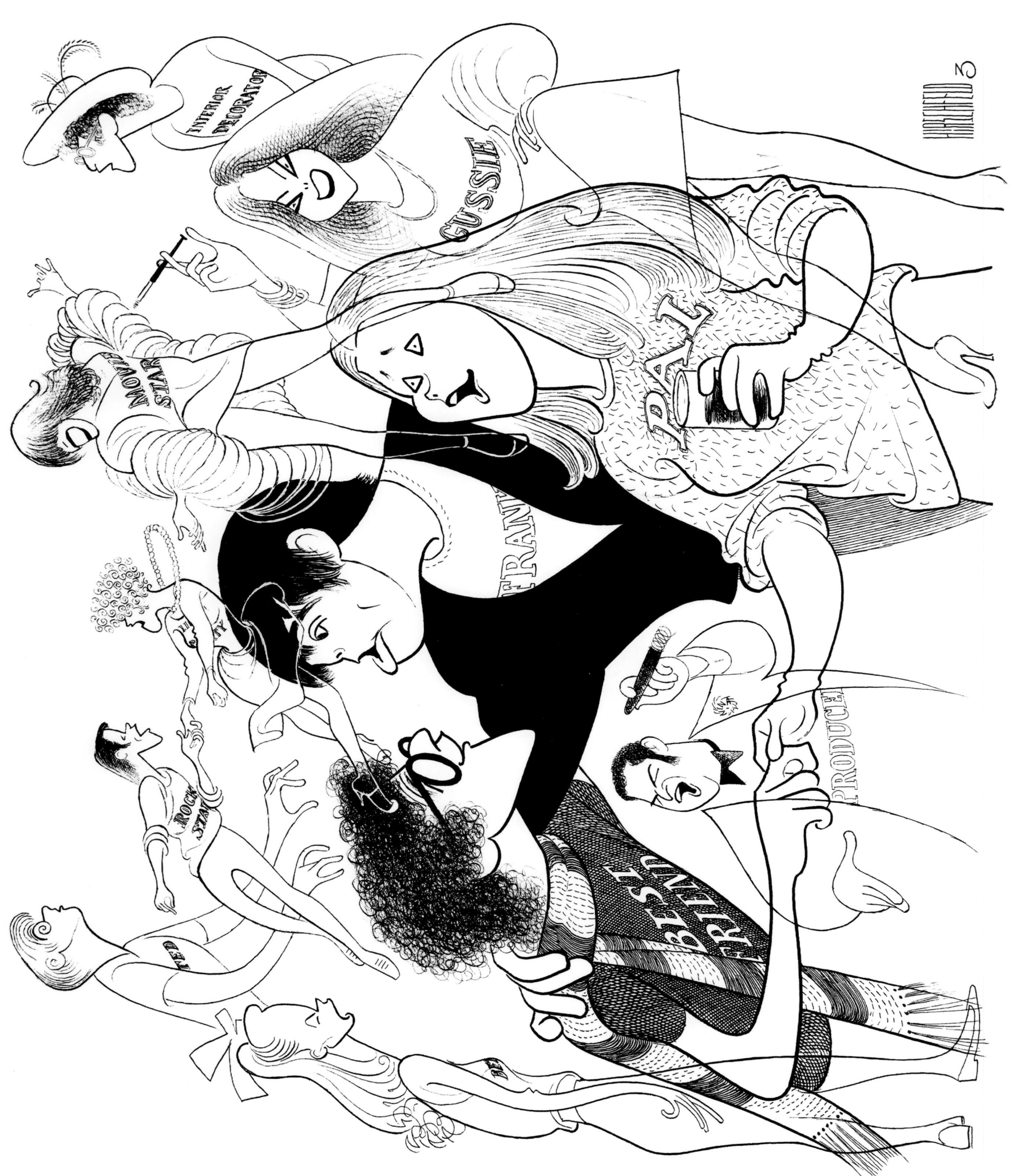

MERRILY WE ROLL ALONG

LEFT TO RIGHT: David Loud, Lonny Price, Jason Alexander, James Weissenbach, Sally Klein, Ann Morrison, and Terry Finn

Ink on board, 1981

A revised version of this drawing was published in the *New York Times*, November 15, 1981

Music and lyrics by Stephen Sondheim; book by George Furth, based on the play *Merrily We Roll Along* by George S. Kaufman and Moss Hart

OPENING DATE: November 16, 1981
CLOSING DATE: November 26, 1981
PERFORMANCES ON BROADWAY: 16

Nominated for one Tony Award:
○ Best Original Score

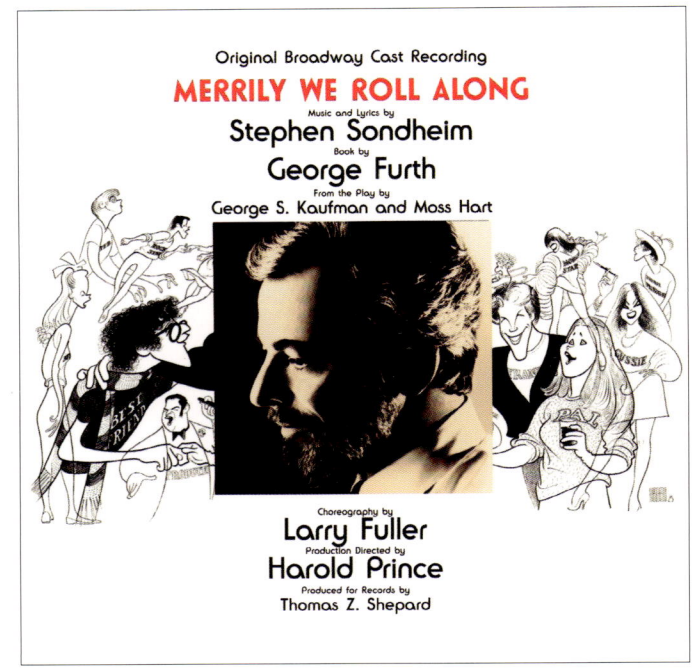

After the success that Hal Prince and Stephen Sondheim had over ten years, it seemed that *Merrily We Roll Along* would add a few more Tonys to their shelves. The play is based on the 1934 George S. Kaufman and Moss Hart comedy about three friends who start out young and idealistic but as they age become jaded and cynical. The twist is that the story is told backward, and the unique framing seemed ideal for Sondheim and Prince. Audiences did not agree. The difficult work of refining the show was done in previews on Broadway rather than out-of-town tryouts, and soon gossip columnists were writing of the set, costume, and even cast changes, as well as audience walkouts. Prince and Sondheim's success with unconventional works may have perturbed the Broadway community, and now they seemed gleeful about the partnership having a flop. The show closed after sixteen performances, and it took the pleading of Sondheim to RCA to honor the commitment to record the score. That cast album kept the show alive for many, and the authors continued to work on it in subsequent productions in regional theaters and the West End. It finally became a Broadway hit forty-three years later after Sondheim, Furth, and Prince had all passed, with a revival starring Daniel Radcliffe, Jonathan Groff, and Lindsay Mendez in October 2023, which went on to win four Tony Awards, including Best Revival of a Musical.

The original cast album from 1981 featured a Hirschfeld drawing on the cover. But the image used, and indeed the one that appeared in the *Times*, was not as Hirschfeld had originally drawn it. Right before opening night the producers fired the leading man, James Weissenbach, and replaced him with another young performer from the cast, Jim Walton. The *Times* wanted the drawing to reflect the show that was to open the night after the drawing ran, so Hirschfeld drew the head of Walton and glued it over Weissenbach's head. Shown here is the drawing as originally conceived.

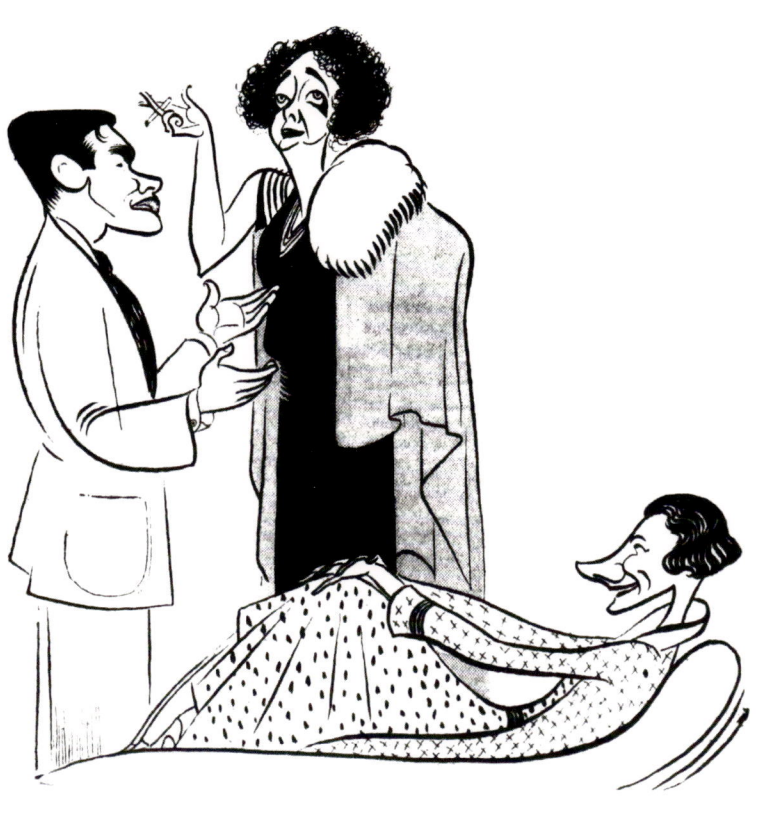

ABOVE
Cast album cover for RCA Records, 1981

LEFT
Merrily We Roll Along (original play)
LEFT TO RIGHT: Walter Abel, Cecilia Loftus, and Mary Philips, 1934

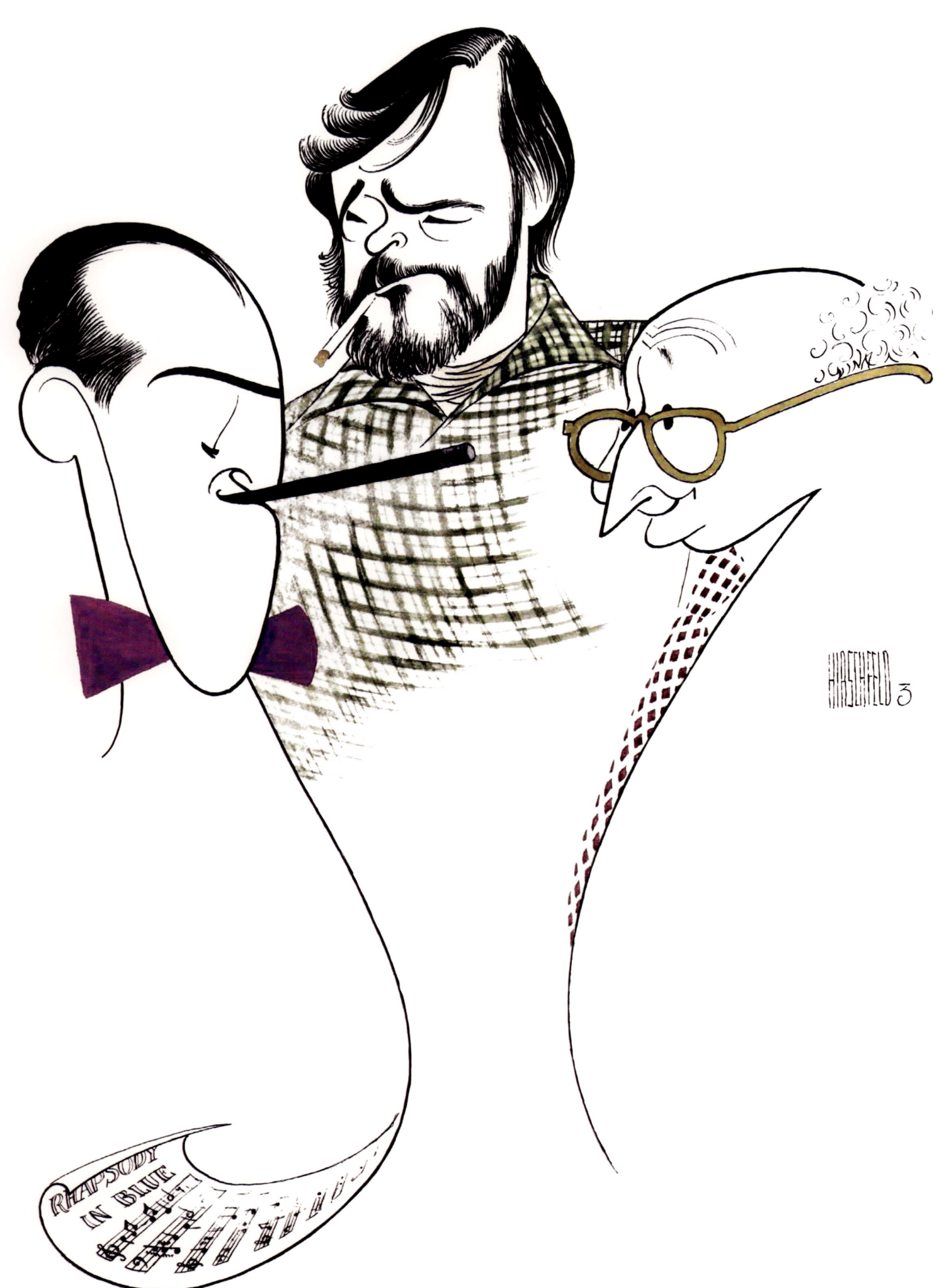

GEORGE GERSHWIN, STEPHEN SONDHEIM, and JEROME KERN

Ink and watercolor on board

Undated and previously unpublished

Sondheim studied the music of both George Gershwin and Jerome Kern when he was a student of composer Milton Babbitt in 1950. Together, Babbitt and Sondheim would dissect their songs and those of others in the musical theater canon just as much as they explored Beethoven and Mozart. When Sondheim became the first visiting professor of contemporary music at Oxford University in 1990, he presented an analysis of Kern's "All the Things You Are" that drew on his work with Babbitt. As for Gershwin, while opera companies have occasionally performed Sondheim's scores, the composer himself was not a fan of opera, although he did like the works of Puccini and Britten, and Gershwin's *Porgy and Bess*.

It is unknown why this work was created. Apparently, a private collector commissioned Hirschfeld to create this drawing of three of the most important theater composers of the twentieth century, who very likely were their favorites. Hirschfeld knew all three men but was closest to Gershwin, whom he grew up with in Washington Heights. It was Hirschfeld who introduced Gershwin to Oscar Levant, who would become a leading Gershwin interpreter. Hirschfeld's first (of many) album covers was of selections from *Porgy and Bess* for Victor Records (1940).

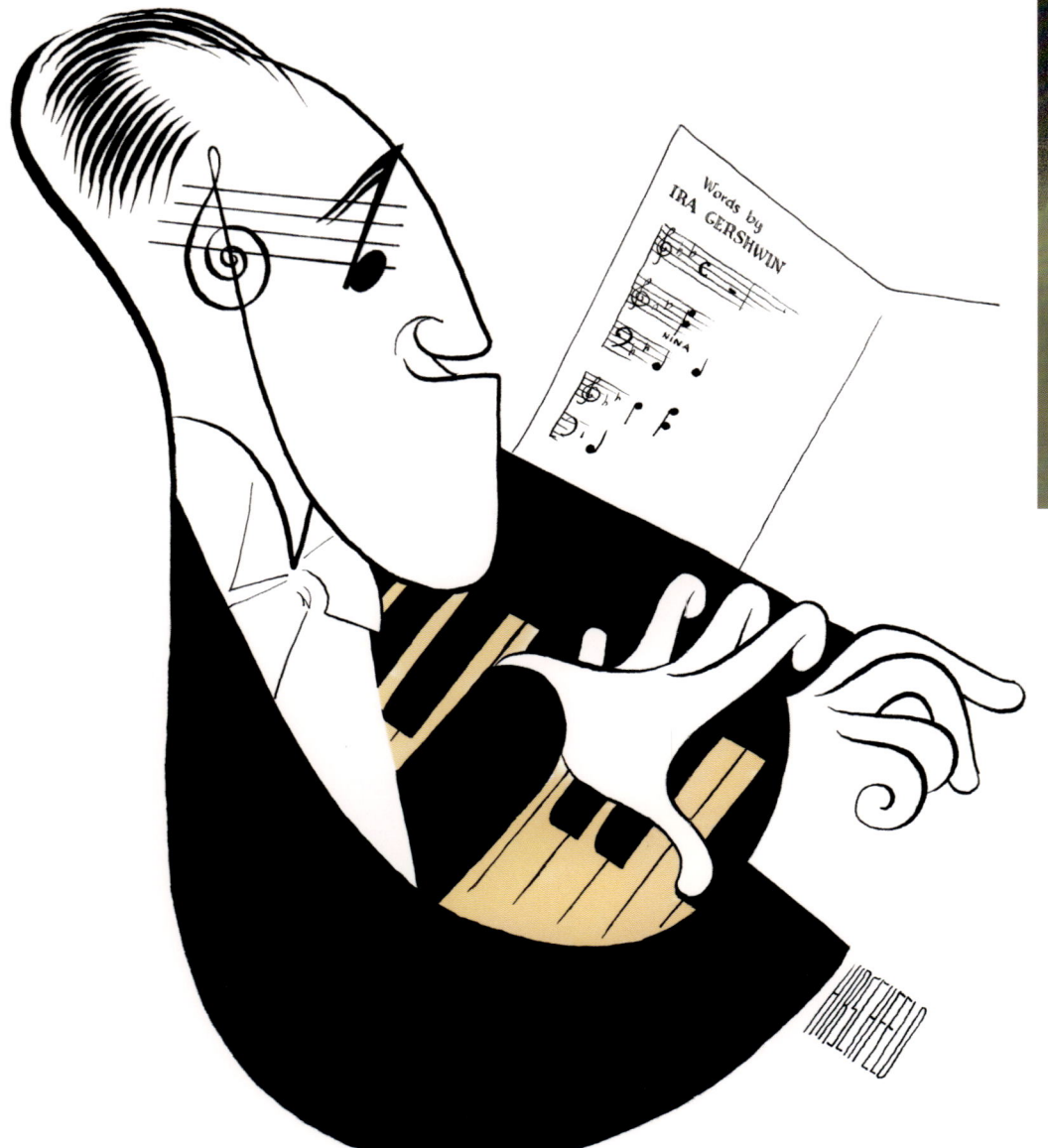

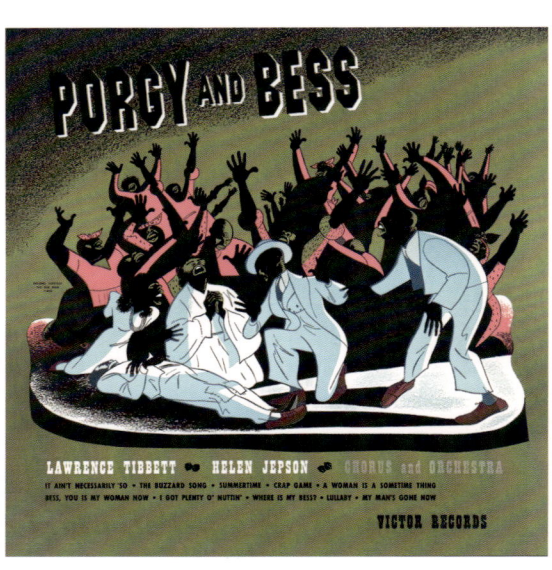

ABOVE
Porgy and Bess album cover,
Victor Records, 1940

LEFT
George Gershwin, 1946

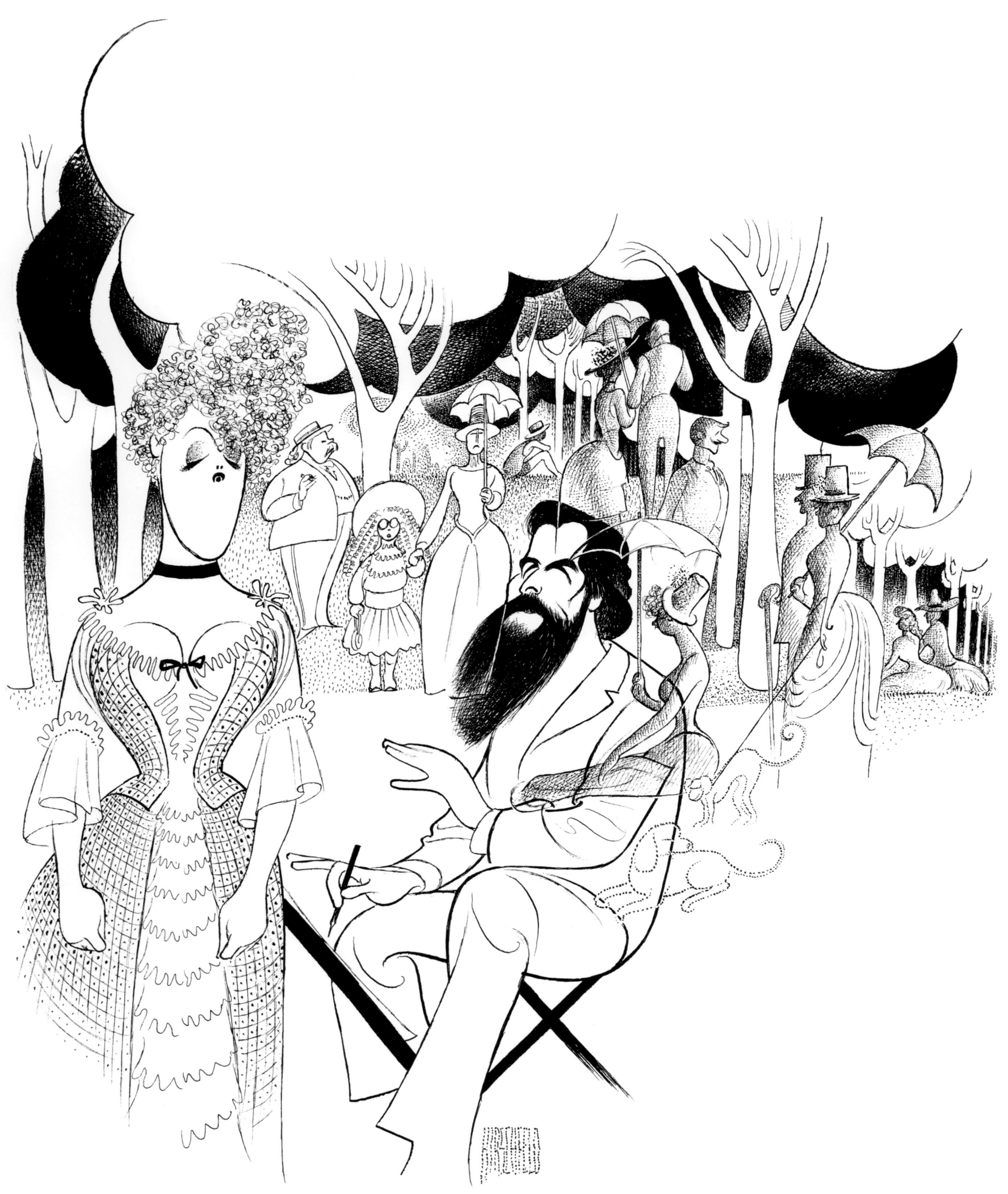

SUNDAY IN THE PARK WITH GEORGE

Bernadette Peters and Mandy Patinkin

Ink on board, 1984

First published in the *New York Times*, April 29, 1984

Music and lyrics by Stephen Sondheim;
book by James Lapine

OPENING DATE: May 2, 1984
CLOSING DATE: October 13, 1985
PERFORMANCES ON BROADWAY: 604

Nominated for ten Tony Awards, it won two:
○ Best Scenic Design: Tony Straiges
○ Best Lighting Design: Richard Nelson

In weekly meetings before they started to write this musical, Sondheim wrote the following note: "The show is, in part, about how creation takes on a life of its own, how artists feed off art (we off Seurat); the artist's relationship to his material." Sondheim had seen how he started with one idea for a show and watched it metamorphosize into something much richer. He had seen his songs, written specifically for a situation/character in a musical, become standards in cabaret. He had routinely been inspired by the work of other artists, whether it be visual or musical. He was also a man of the theater, so much so that he felt that even though he was producing some of his best work, he was a dinosaur, since he came of age during what is considered the Golden Age of the Broadway musical.

Hirschfeld could have described his work very similarly. He took sketches made in the dark and transmuted them into a composition on hot press board that he essentially improvised as he drew. He fed off the performing arts, and theater here specifically, which supplied him with an endless array of subjects and situations to turn into a drawing that he said "would stand on its own two feet." Hirschfeld had a long-term relationship with the American theater, having drawn it since 1926. His passion for the art form never waned.

Robert Westenberg in *Sunday in the Park with George*, 1984

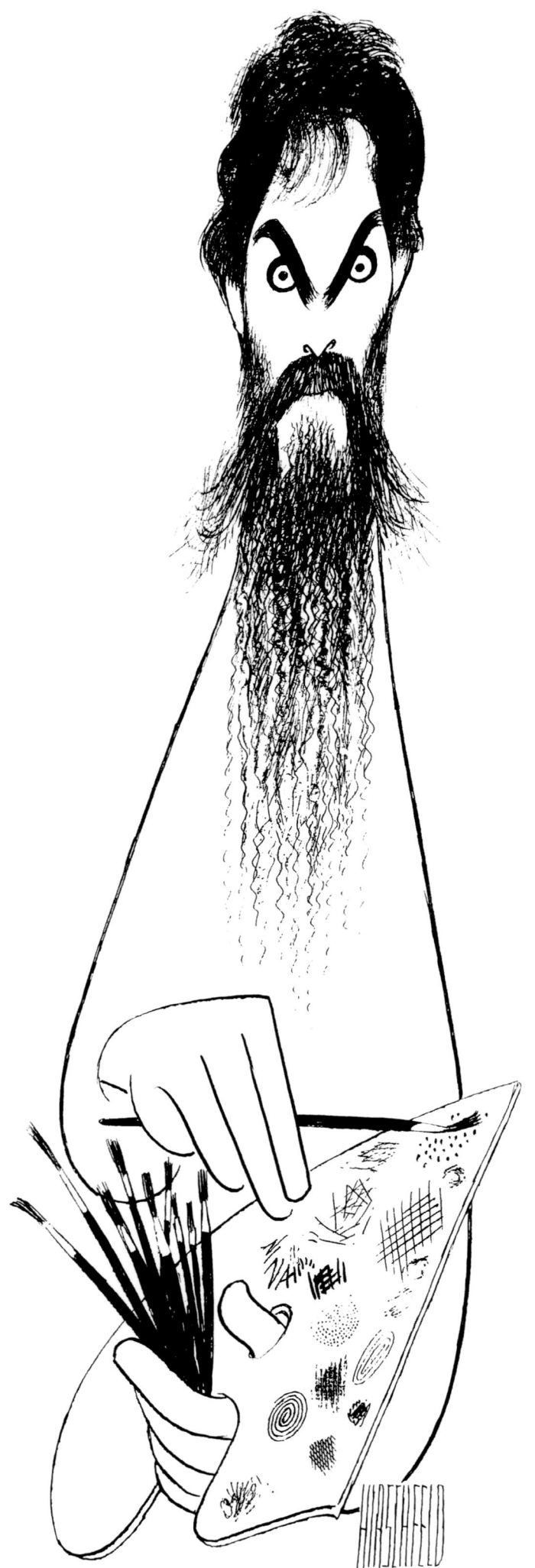

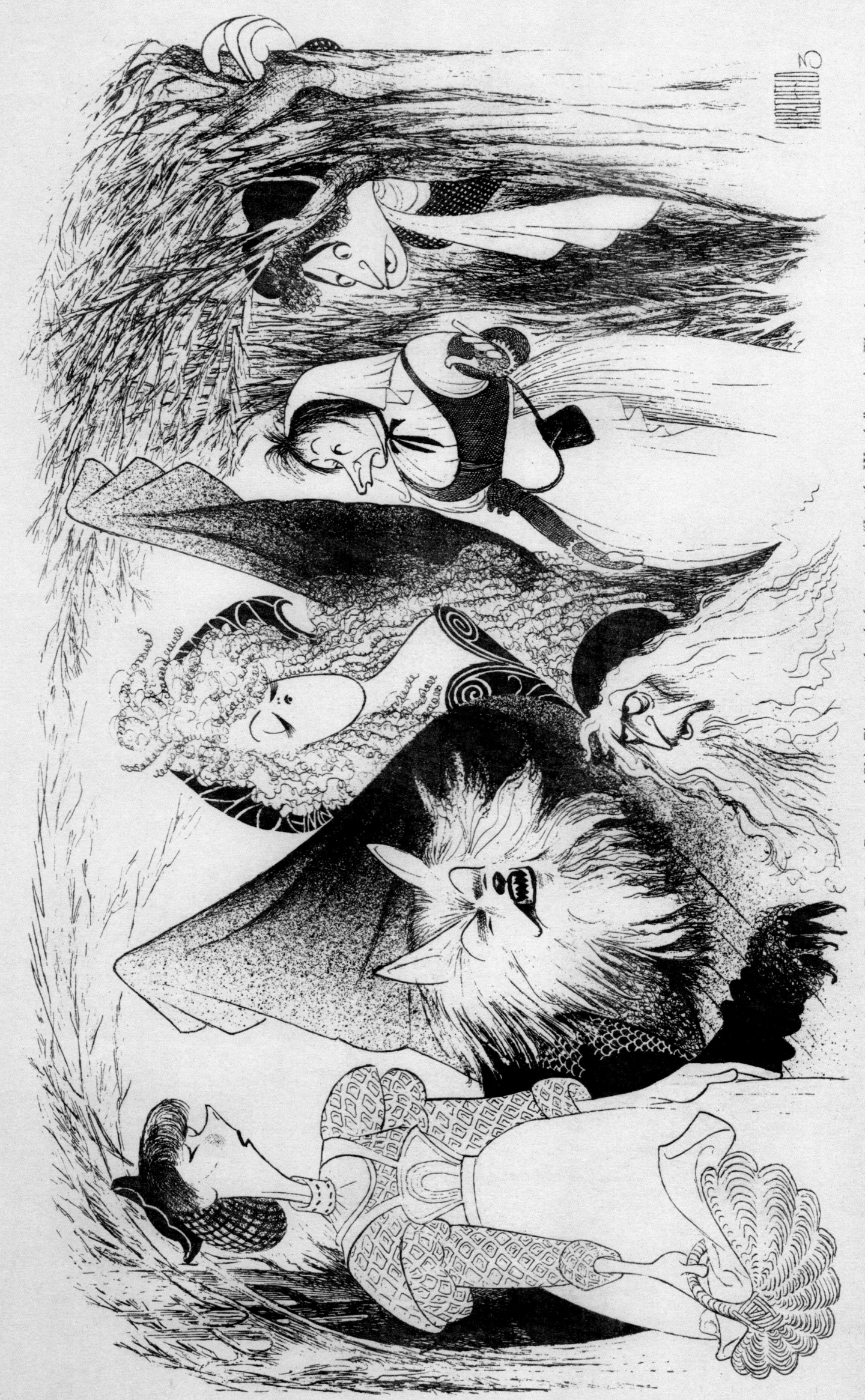

Joanna Gleason, Robert Westenberg, Tom Aldredge, Bernadette Peters, Barbara Bryne and Chip Zien as storybook characters in "Into the Woods," opening Thursday at the Martin Beck Theater

INTO THE WOODS

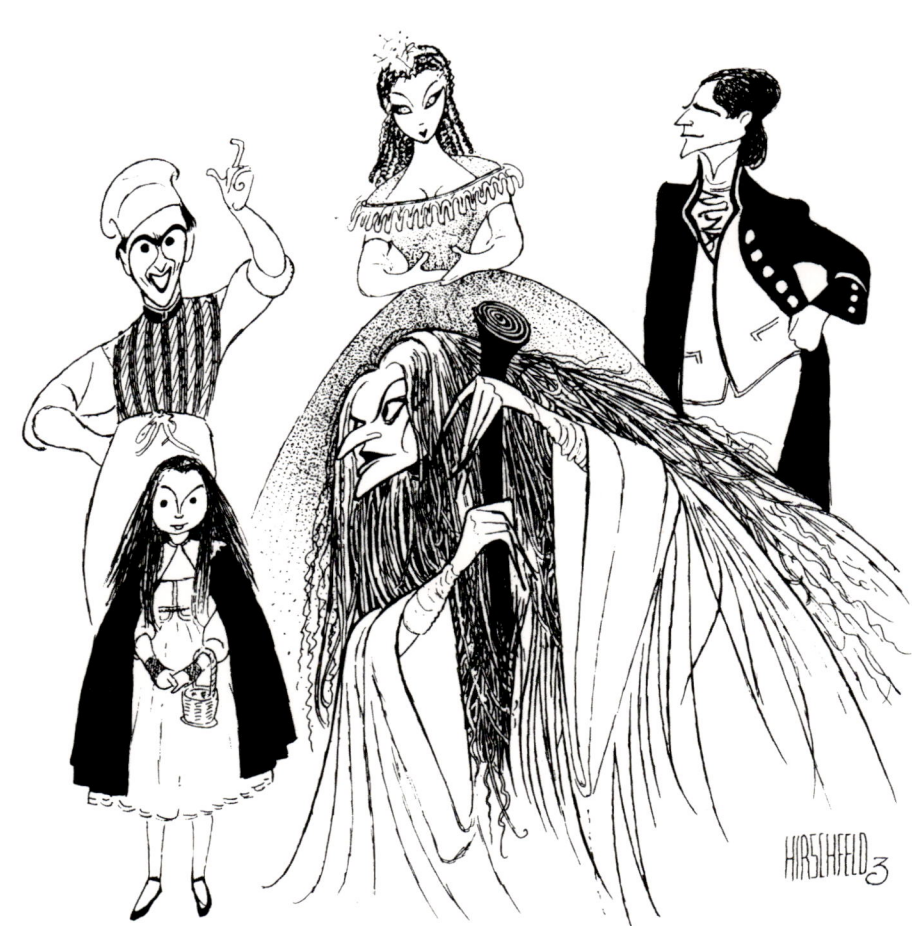

LEFT TO RIGHT: Joanna Gleason, Robert Westenberg, Tom Aldredge, Bernadette Peters, Barbara Byrne, and Chip Zien

Newspaper clipping

First published in the *New York Times*, November 1, 1987

Music and lyrics by Stephen Sondheim; book by James Lapine

OPENING DATE: November 5, 1987
CLOSING DATE: September 3, 1989
PERFORMANCES ON BROADWAY: 765

Nominated for ten Tony Awards, it won three:
○ Best Original Score
○ Best Book of a Musical
○ Best Actress in a Musical: Joanna Gleason

Hirschfeld's drawings first appeared in newspapers as early as 1921. His first published caricature was in 1925, and his first theatrical caricature was published in 1926. Although his work appeared in many types of publications, as well as on posters, programs, album covers, book covers, and eventually postage stamps, his best-known works appeared in newspapers for nine decades, primarily in the *New York Times*, where his art was published, on average, every other week for seventy-five years. Hirschfeld breathed new life into newspaper illustrations by making his art dance, twirl, and high kick across the page, producing lively drawings of the lively arts. Unlike many of his contemporaries, his art was a stand-alone feature that rarely accompanied an article or review. Although his career would go into the twenty-first century, all of Hirschfeld's work first appeared in printed form.

After the success of *Sunday in the Park with George*, Sondheim and Lapine were interested in a quest story like *The Wizard of Oz*, and they also breathed new life into an ancient art form, the

fairy tale, by having characters from several classic stories collide with one another to help tell a new fairy tale that the authors invented. In the nineteenth century, Jacob and Wilhelm Grimm researched tales from the oral tradition and collected them into a book, *Children's and Household Tales*. Their book included stories of Cinderella, Hansel and Gretel, Little Red Riding Hood, Rapunzel, and Sleeping Beauty, to name a few. *Into the Woods* would take these ancient tales and refashion them for audiences in the late twentieth century.

ABOVE
Into the Woods (revival)

CLOCKWISE FROM BOTTOM LEFT: Molly Ephraim, Stephen De Ross, Laura Benanti, Gregg Edelman, and Vanessa Williams, 2002

RIGHT
Poster for the MGM film *The Wizard of Oz*, 1939. Hirschfeld designed four of the six posters for the original release of the film, including this one where the story is summarized in the letters of the title.

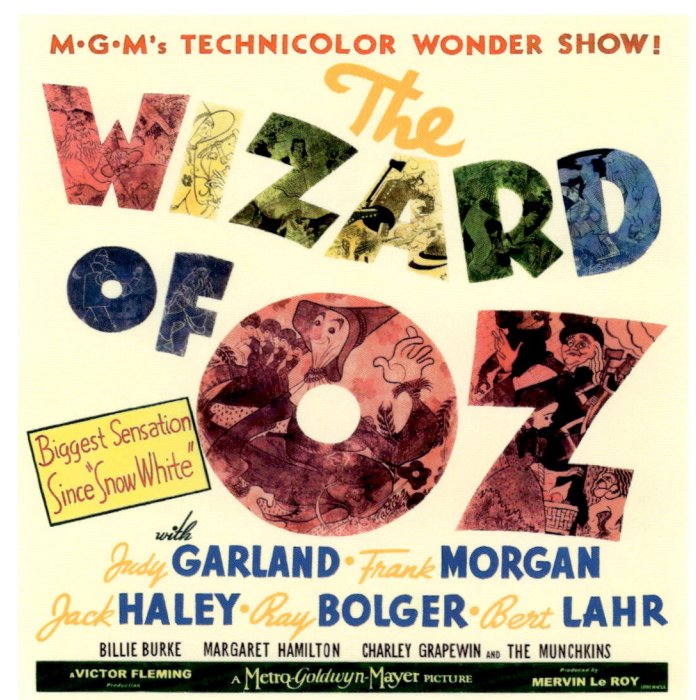

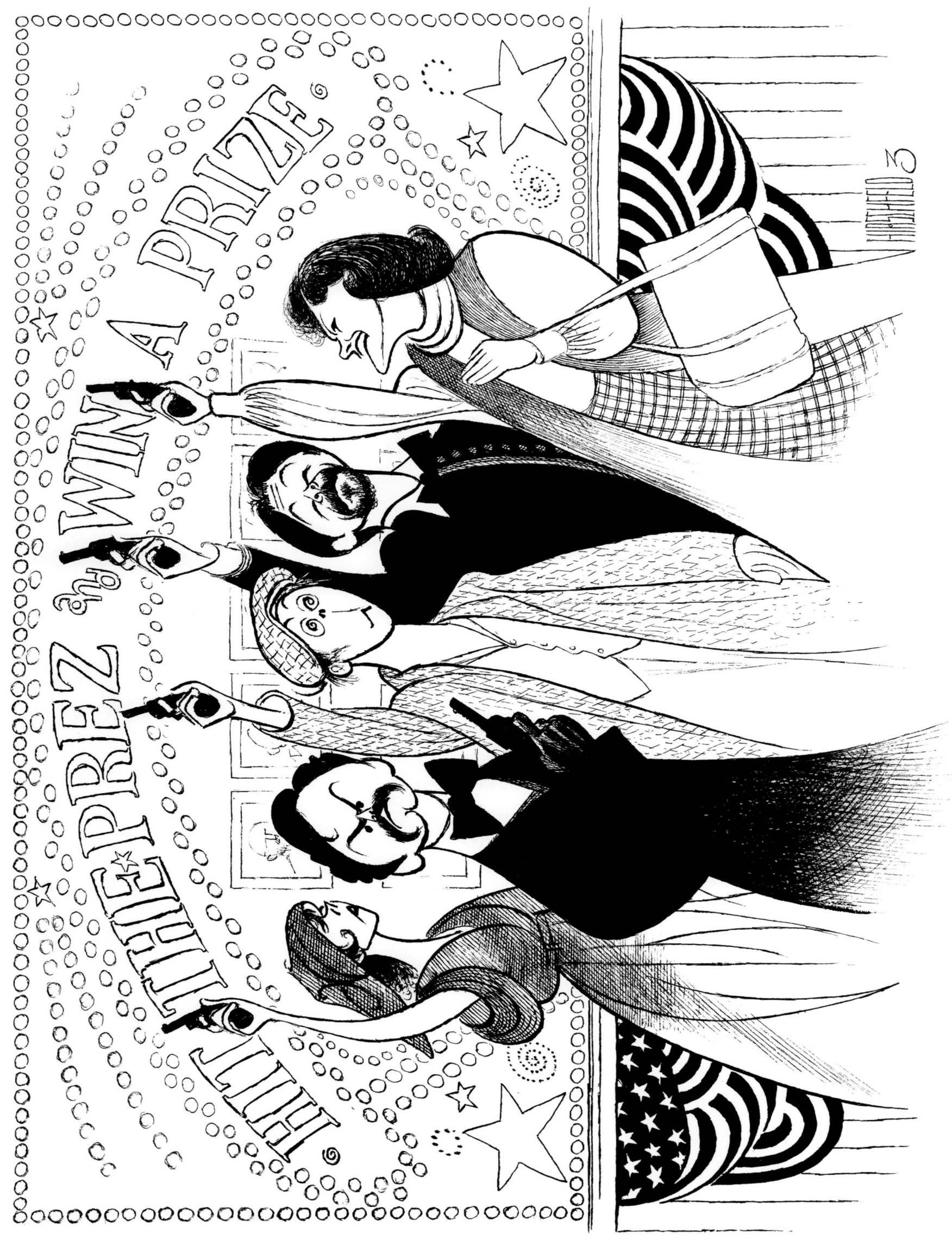

ASSASSINS

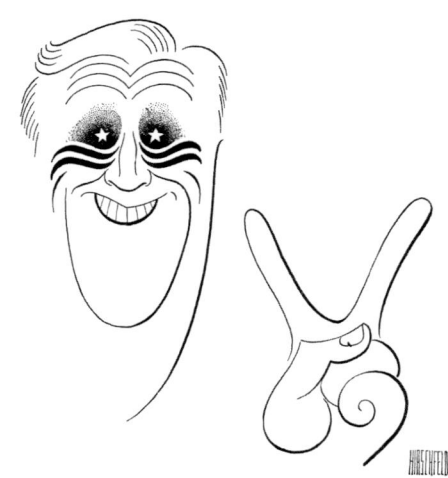

LEFT TO RIGHT: Debra Monk, Victor Garber, Jonathan Hadary, Terrence Mann, and Annie Golden

Ink on board, 1991

First published in the *New York Times*, January 27, 1991

Music and lyrics by Stephen Sondheim; book by John Weidman, based on an idea by Charles Gilbert Jr.

OPENING DATE: December 18, 1990
CLOSING DATE: February 16, 1991
Performances Off-Broadway: 71

Assassins features nine of the thirteen people who have tried to assassinate the president of the United States at the time. Originally, Sondheim and Weidman thought they might include assassins from world history going back to at least Brutus. But when that idea proved unwieldy, they decided to focus only on US presidential assassins.

Although the presidents themselves play no role in the show, Hirschfeld had his own interactions with White House residents. In 1965, he had drawn a composite of fourteen performers who appeared as part of President Lyndon Johnson's inauguration at the instigation of composer Richard Adler, who produced the event. Johnson was not a favorite of Hirschfeld's, who said, "He impressed me as an affable drummer covering the southwest territory for a slick New York cigar manufacturer." With the drawing completed, the Hirschfeld family was invited to the Oval Office

on March 9, 1965, so that he could gift the new president with the piece. He went reluctantly, not only because of his tepid response to Johnson, but also because Hirschfeld swore off meeting any world leaders after a previous visit to the White House to meet Franklin D. Roosevelt, when he gave him a drawing that appeared on the cover of the *Nation* in 1944. Roosevelt, whom Hirschfeld revered, had appeared so decidedly human that he concluded, "I was thankful that I never met President Lincoln."

Nevertheless, while in the Oval Office, Johnson put a telephone call on speakerphone, and soon the room reverberated with his conversation with Martin Luther King Jr. King was at the Edmund Pettus Bridge in Selma, Alabama, with 2,500 supporters but blocked by state troopers and the Ku Klux Klan. He was bent on crossing the bridge. "I understand, Dr. King, and please tell them that their president is with them in spirit," said Johnson. "I can only advise them to hold the line and avoid the spilling of more blood. May God be with you." Hirschfeld was impressed as their fifteen-minute interview stretched into an hour, and Johnson talked of the moral dilemma of sending more troops to Vietnam. Hirschfeld was so engrossed that he never took out his pencil to sketch the president. His opinion of Johnson would change. "The cigar salesman turned into that of a warm, lovable, and confused grandmother."

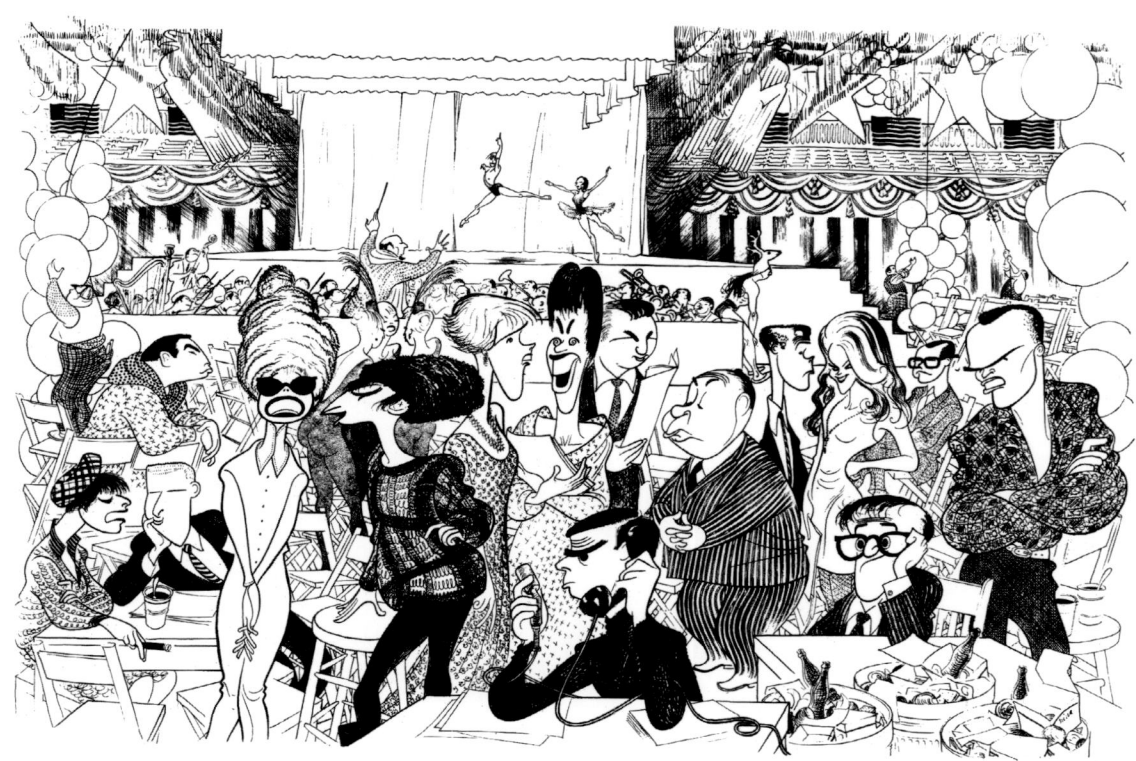

ABOVE
Franklin Roosevelt, 1944

LEFT

Johnson Inauguration Washington Gala

LEFT TO RIGHT: Elaine May, Mike Nichols, Carol Channing, Barbra Streisand, Julie Andrews, Carol Burnett, Margot Fonteyn, Rudolf Nureyev, Bobby Darin, Richard Adler, Alfred Hitchcock, Johnny Carson, Ann-Margret, Woody Allen, and Harry Belafonte, 1965

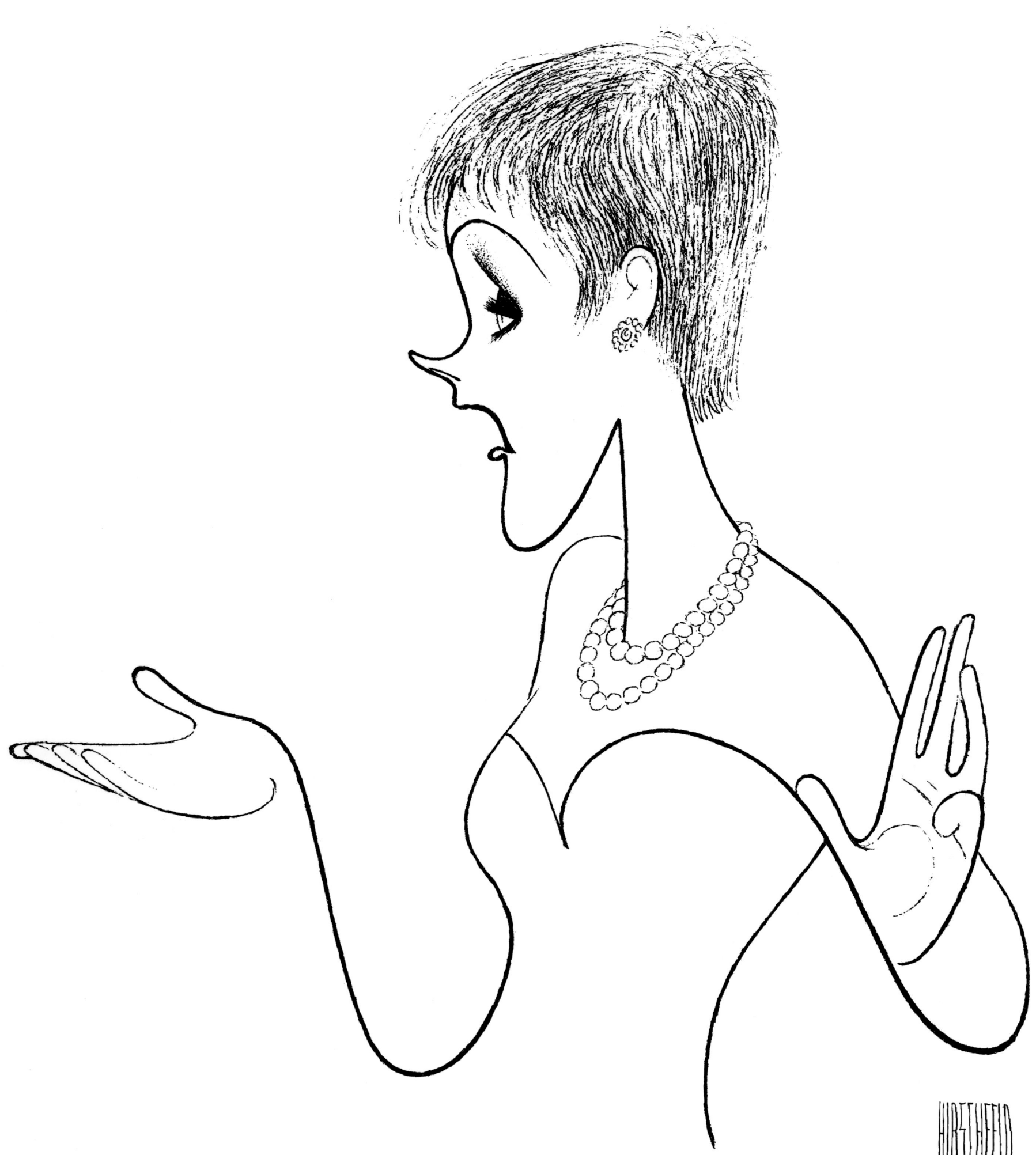

JULIE ANDREWS in PUTTING IT TOGETHER

Ink on board, 1993

First published in the *New York Times*, March 28, 1993

Music and lyrics by Stephen Sondheim;
original 1992 production devised by
Stephen Sondheim and Julia McKenzie

OPENING DATE: March 2, 1993
CLOSING DATE: May 23, 1993
PERFORMANCES OFF-BROADWAY: 96

Like *Side by Side by Sondheim*, the first revue of Sondheim songs, *Putting It Together*, started in England. Julia McKenzie, one of the stars and co-creators of the original revue, who had just directed a successful production of *Merrily We Roll Along* in England, put it together with Sondheim's input. Once again it was produced by Cameron Mackintosh, who had just produced a new revival of *Follies* in the West End. *Putting It Together* starred Diana Rigg in London, and when it came to America, Julie Andrews took on the role. It was Andrews's first time back on a New York stage since *Camelot* in 1960.

Hirschfeld had been drawing Andrews since her debut on Broadway, in *The Boy Friend*, in 1955. His poster of her and Rex Harrison for the original production of *My Fair Lady* has become one of the most recognizable pieces of Broadway iconography. Hirschfeld would continue to draw Andrews as she left the stage for film, resulting in fifty-five drawings over forty-seven years, the most drawings he created of any actress in his career. "When Hirschfeld drew a likeness of me, he always made my chin quite pronounced—even slack jawed," remembered Andrews. "This began, I believe, during the *My Fair Lady* years when my portrayal of Eliza, as a cockney girl, did have a somewhat slack-jawed air. And I guess the impression stuck! Some thirty or forty years later—by which time the chin had definitely filled out—Tony Walton tactfully suggested to Hirschfeld that he modify the likeness a bit and the dear man did!"

TOP
Cameron Mackintosh manipulates the cast
and creative team of *Putting It Together*, 1993.

BOTTOM
Camelot

LEFT TO RIGHT: Richard Burton, Julie Andrews,
Robert Goulet, and Roddy McDowall, 1960

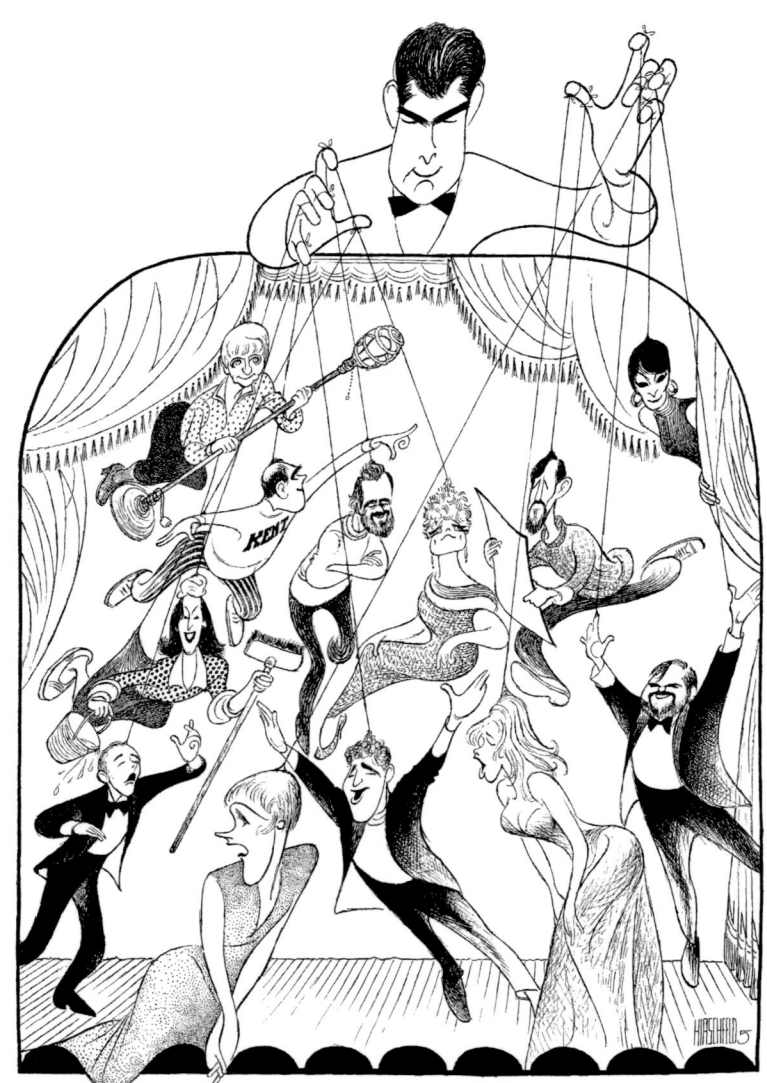

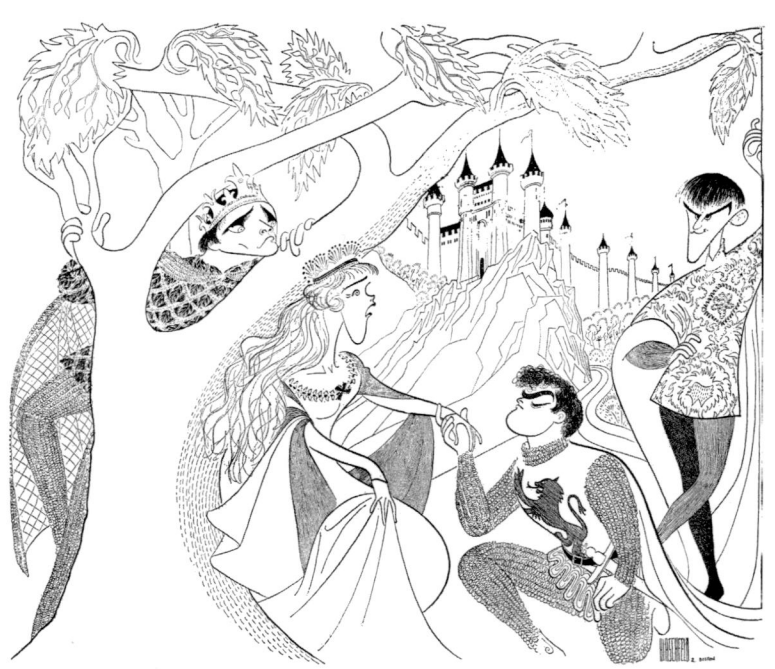

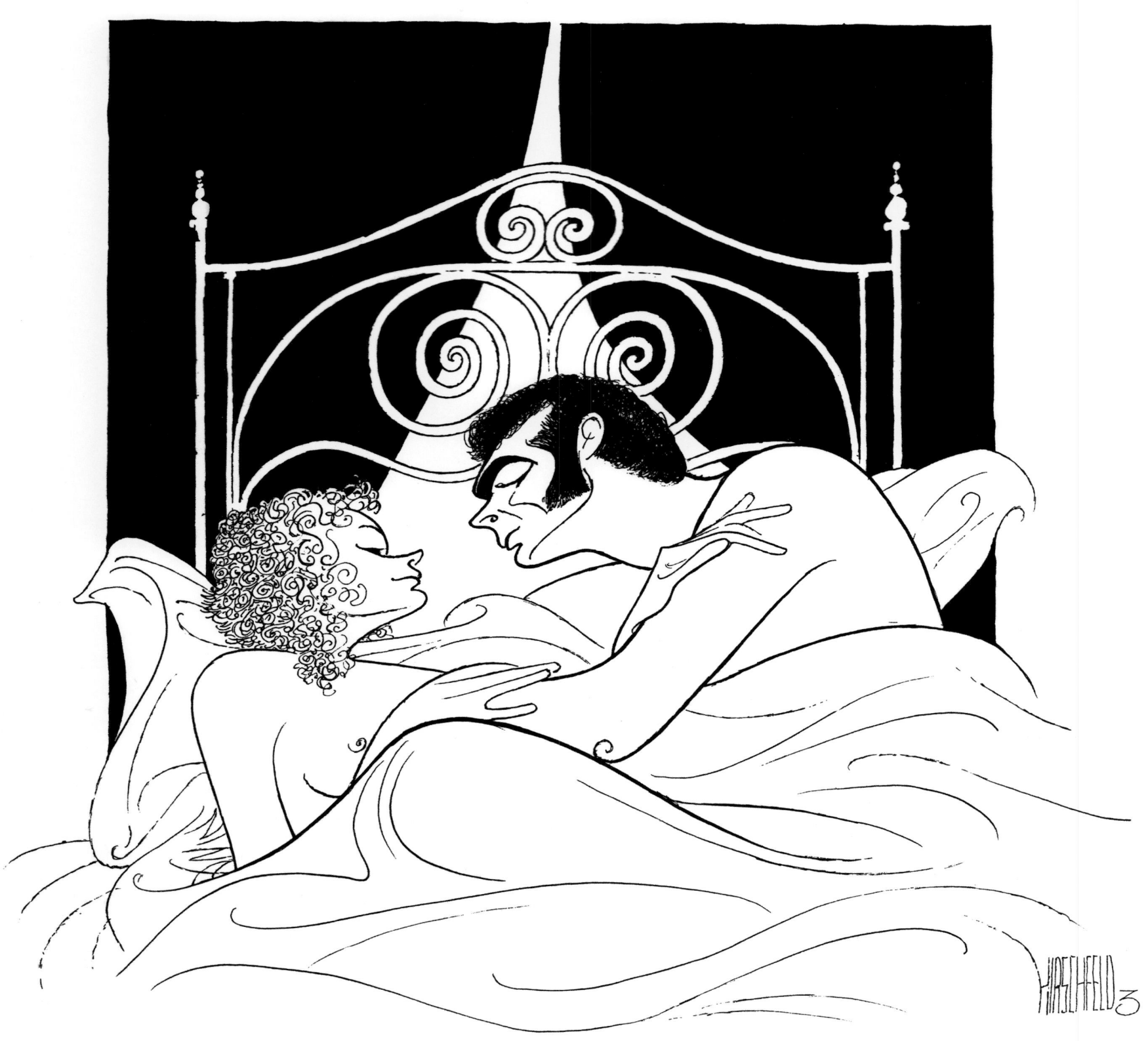

PASSION

Marin Mazzie and Jere Shea

Ink on board, 1994

Music and lyrics by Stephen Sondheim;
book by James Lapine, based on the novel *Fosca* by
Iginio Ugo Tarchetti and the film *Passione d'Amore*

OPENING DATE: May 9, 1994
CLOSING DATE: January 7, 1995
PERFORMANCES ON BROADWAY: 280

Nominated for ten Tony Awards, it won four:
○ Best Musical
○ Best Original Score
○ Best Book of a Musical
○ Best Actress in a Musical: Donna Murphy

When Hirschfeld sent in his drawing for *Passion* to his editor at the *New York Times*, an unusual thing happened—it was rejected. Hirschfeld claimed it was because the paper was uncomfortable that his drawing discreetly showed Marin Mazzie's nipple. This was not Hirschfeld's first note along these lines. Forty years earlier, he drew the logo image for Harvey Kunitz's satire on art collectors and dealers, *Reclining Figure*, which showed a lounging nude with a scarf covering her lower half. The *Times* insisted he put a bra on the figure before they would publish any advertisements with the image.

The more likely reason the drawing of Marin Mazzie and Jere Shea was rejected was because it failed to include Fosca, whose passion is the centerpiece of the musical. She is "an unattractive and aggressive young woman given to fits of hysteria" who falls in love in with and relentlessly pursues the handsome young captain in the Italian army, Giorgio, who is having an affair with a beautiful married woman, Clara. Hirschfeld created a new work with all three characters that proved to be so popular it was later published as a limited-edition lithograph.

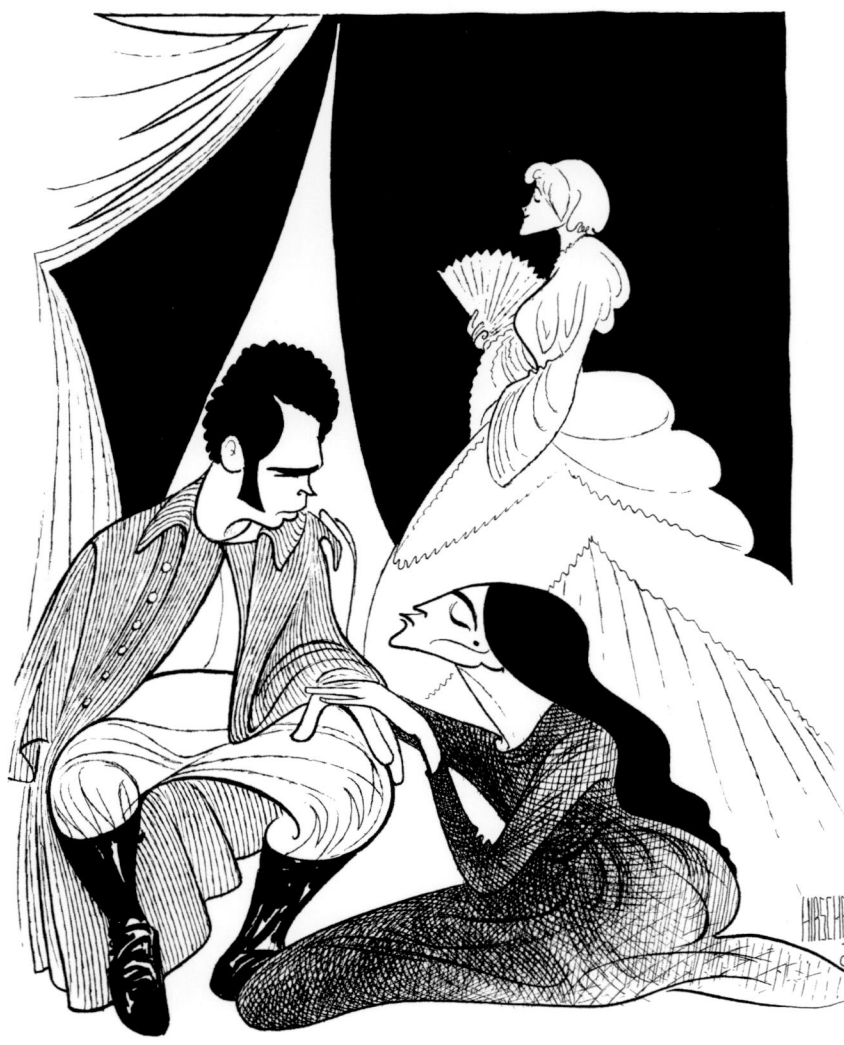

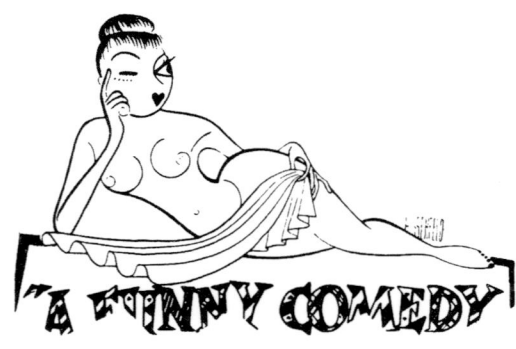

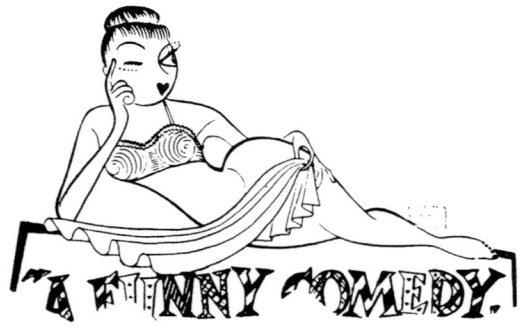

ABOVE
Reclining Figure (censored and uncensored versions), 1954

LEFT
Passion

LEFT TO RIGHT: Jere Shea, Donna Murphy, and Marin Mazzie (standing), 1994

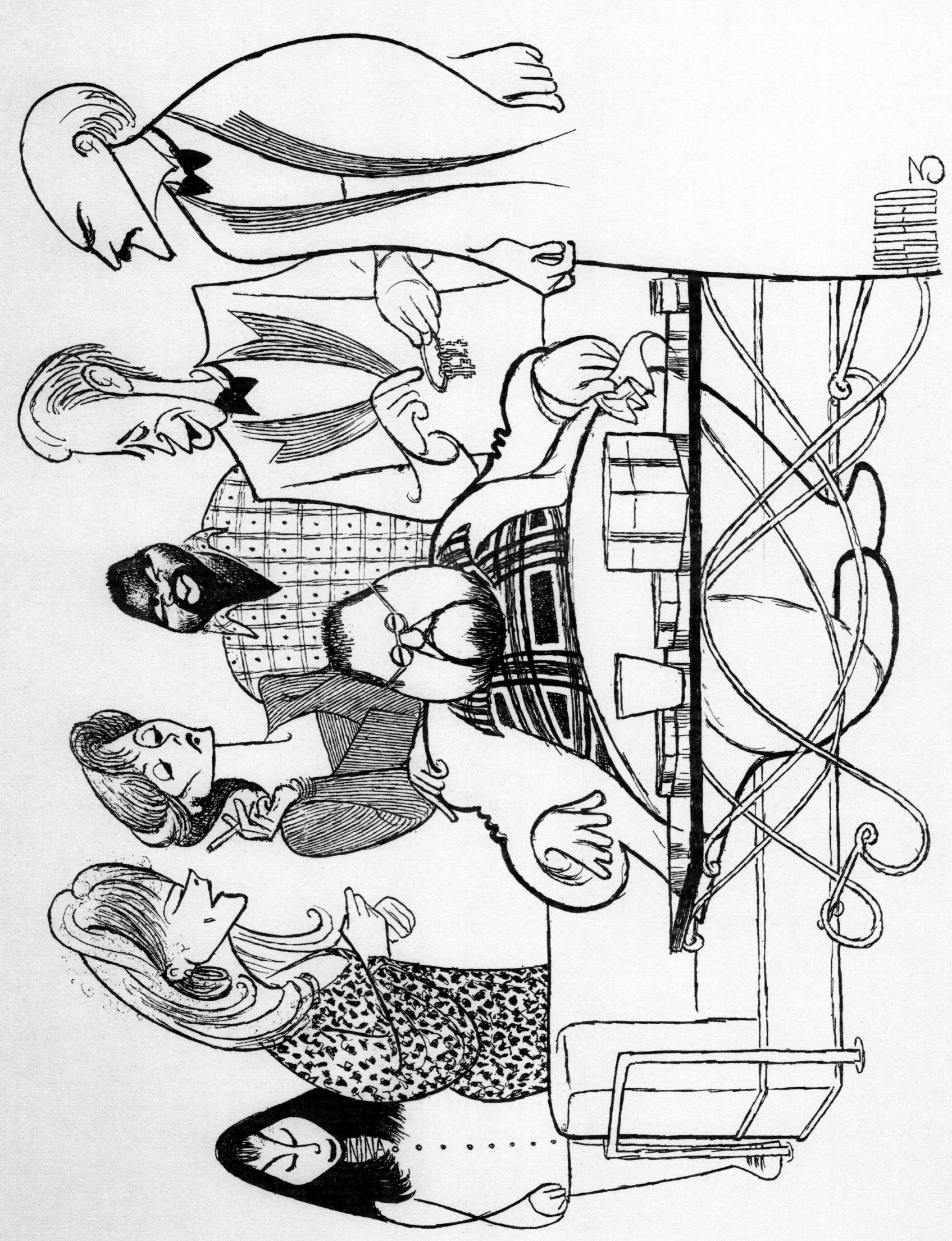

Jodi Long, far left, Christine Ebersole, Kandis Chappell, Frankie R. Faison, Terrence Mann, John Rubinstein and, seated, Josh Mostel in "Getting Away With Murder," by Stephen Sondheim and George Furth.

GETTING AWAY WITH MURDER

LEFT TO RIGHT: Jodi Long, Christine
Ebersole, Kandis Chappell,
Josh Mostel, Frankie Faison,
Terrence Mann, and John Rubinstein

Newspaper clipping

First published in the *New York
Times*, March 10, 1996

By Stephen Sondheim
and George Furth

OPENING DATE: March 17, 1996
CLOSING DATE: March 31, 1996
PERFORMANCES ON BROADWAY: 17

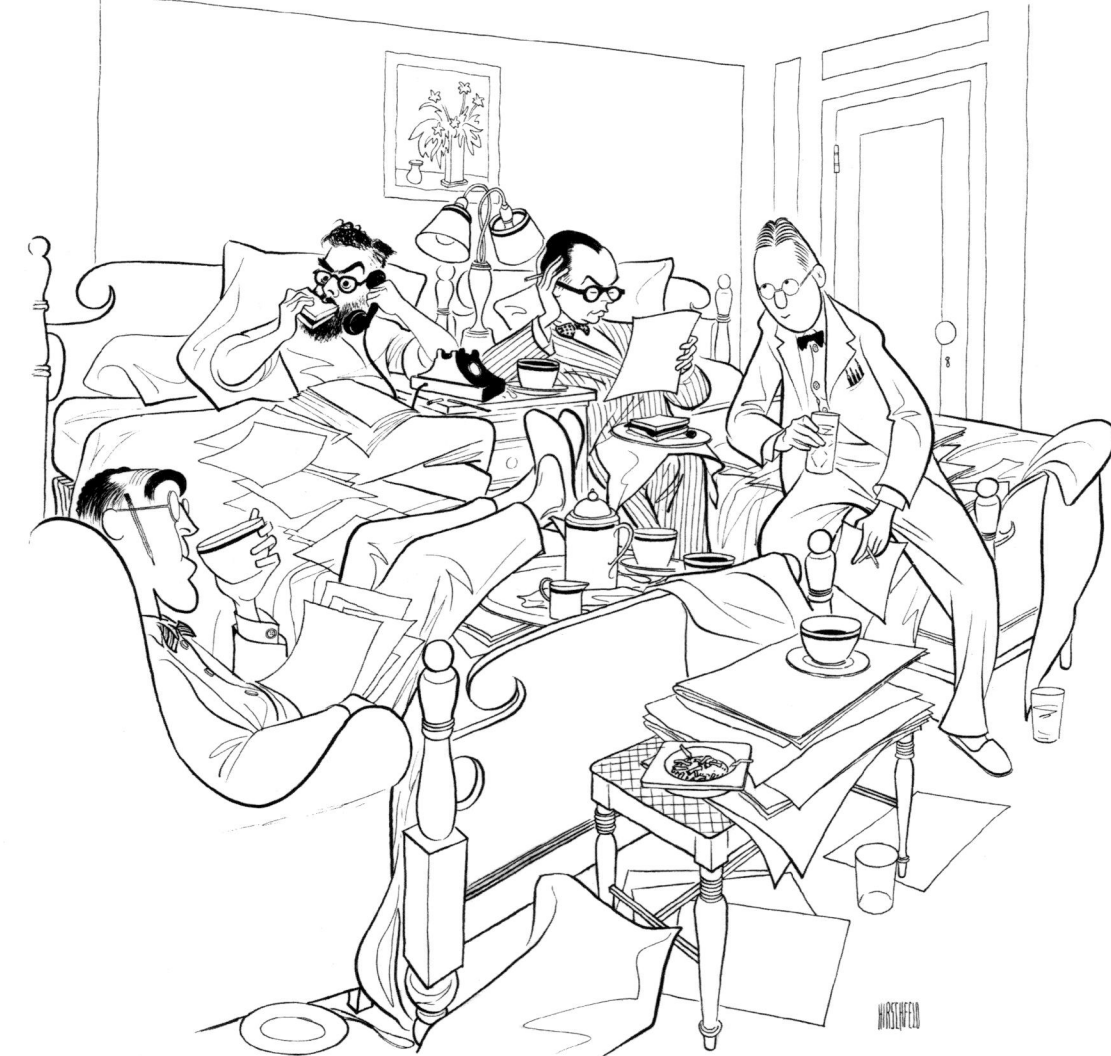

Working on *Sweet Bye and Bye*
(aka "Death in Philadelphia").
LEFT TO RIGHT: S. J. Perelman,
Al Hirschfeld, Ogden Nash,
and Vernon Duke, 1947

In the 1995–96 theater season, the new Sondheim show was a play, not a musical. A lifelong lover of games and mysteries, Sondheim collaborated with George Furth on a comedy thriller about seven patients of an eminent psychiatrist meeting for their weekly group therapy session, only to discover that the doctor has been murdered. The play concerns their own investigation into the crime. Critics were not kind, and the show closed in two weeks.

Hirschfeld could relate. In 1945, humorist S. J. Perelman convinced his old friend Hirschfeld that they should work together on the book of a new musical comedy. Ogden Nash was on board as the lyricist, and Vernon Duke wrote the music. They wrote a satire on advertising and American business set in 2076, when the time capsule of the 1939 New York World's Fair is to be opened, eventually titled *Sweet Bye and Bye*. But what played well on the page did not necessarily translate well to the stage. Hirschfeld claimed the problem was that no one could ever compose music of the future, but Nash, and particularly Duke, never understood the book. It was star-crossed even further when the original leading lady, British actress and singer Pat Kirkwood, had a nervous breakdown in the third week of rehearsals. Vaudevillian Gene Sheldon was chosen for the male lead, except he wasn't a singer, and on the opening night in New Haven he jettisoned the script in the first act and started to perform his vaudeville act. Perelman knocked him out at intermission, with his part played in the second act by the stage manager with script in hand. Sheldon was replaced, but his substitute couldn't remember his lines. The show closed in Philadelphia before reaching New York.

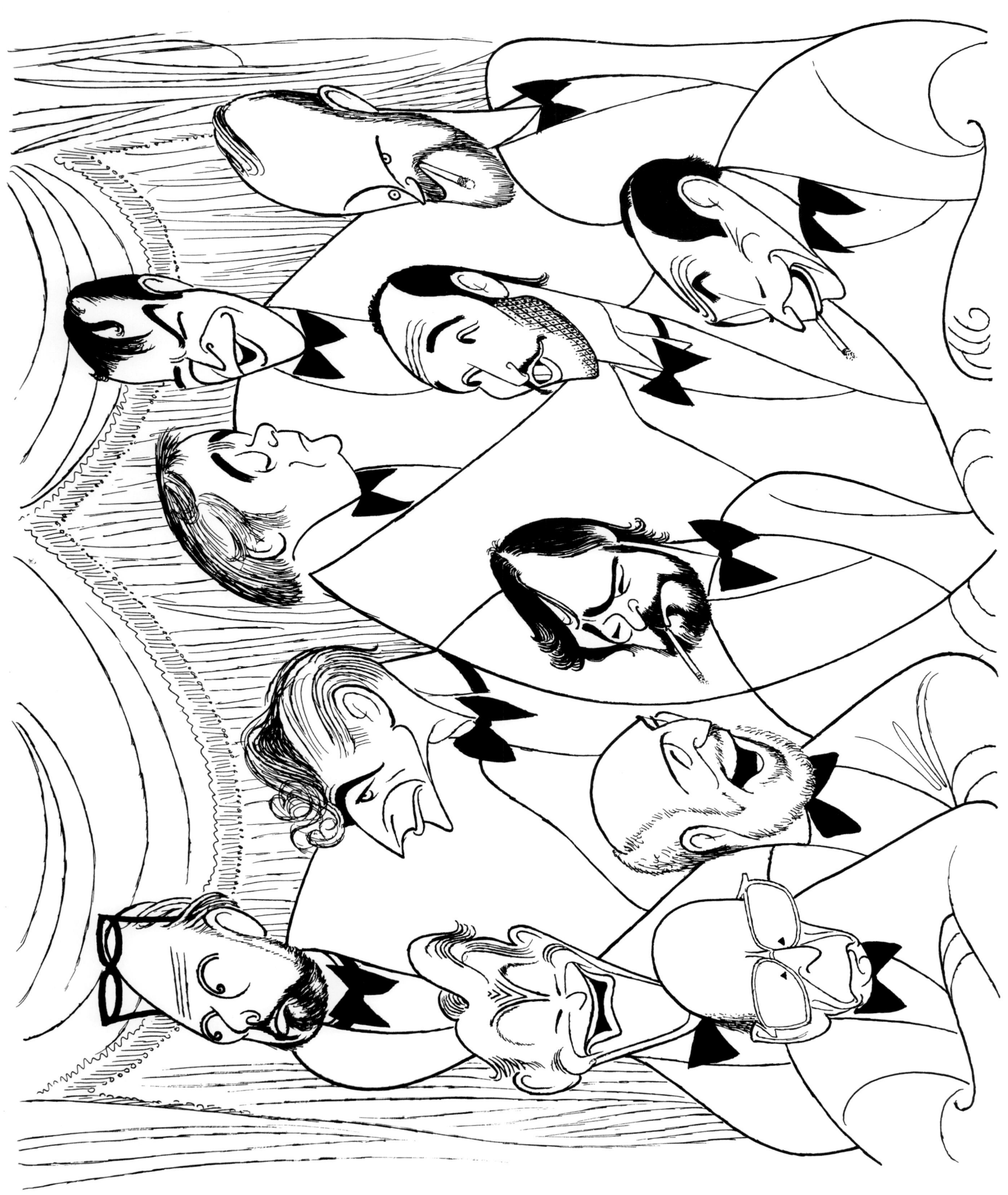

AMERICAN MUSICAL THEATER MURAL (Part 2)

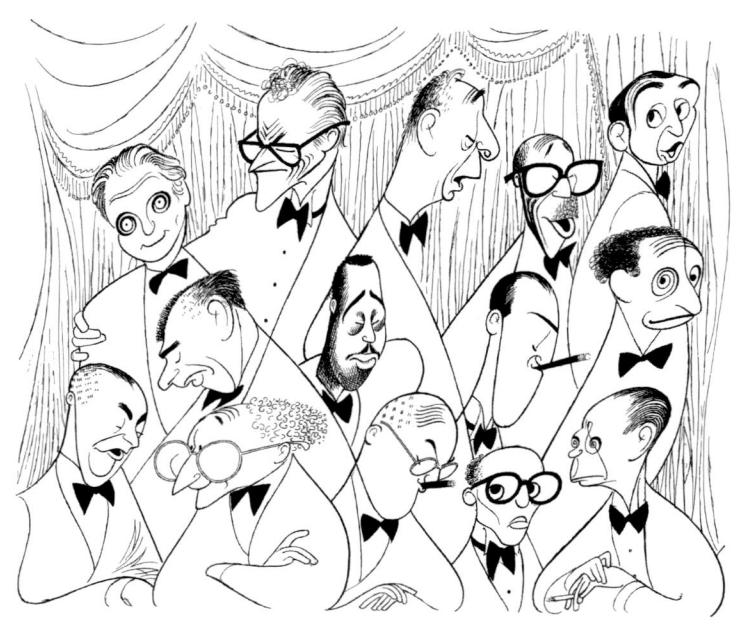

TOP, LEFT TO RIGHT: Harold Prince, Leonard Bernstein, John Kander, Fred Ebb, and Bob Fosse

BOTTOM, LEFT TO RIGHT: Yip Harburg, George Abbott, Jerome Robbins, Stephen Sondheim, Michael Bennett, and Frank Loesser

Ink on board, 1999

Hal Prince's impact on the American theater and the American musical cannot be overstated. Whether producing or directing, Prince was responsible for many milestones in the second half of the twentieth century, starting with *Pajama Game*, *Damn Yankees*, and *West Side Story*. His twenty-one Tonys include producing and/or directing *Fiddler on the Roof*, *Cabaret*, *Zorba*, *Evita*, *Kiss of the Spider Woman*, and one for directing the longest-running show in Broadway history, *The Phantom of the Opera*. In addition to producing *West Side Story* with Sondheim, he also produced *A Funny Thing Happened on the Way to the Forum* and *Side by Side by Sondheim*. He also produced and directed *Company*, *Follies*, *A Little Night Music*, *Pacific Overtures*, *Sweeney Todd*, and *Merrily We Roll Along*.

In 1999, the American Music Theater Festival in Philadelphia moved into a new theater and renamed it, and the organization, the Prince Music Theater in honor of the prolific Prince. The organization commissioned Hirschfeld to create a mural of the most important figures in American musical theater history, and the second of four interconnected panels included both Sondheim and Prince, as well as many of their collaborators.

ABOVE

American Musical Theater Mural (Part 1), 1999

TOP, LEFT TO RIGHT: Frederick Loewe, Oscar Hammerstein, Alan Jay Lerner, Duke Ellington, Burton Lane, George Gershwin, Eubie Blake, Irving Berlin, and Harold Arlen.
BOTTOM, LEFT TO RIGHT: Richard Rodgers, Jerome Kern, Ira Gershwin, Kurt Weill, and Cole Porter

BELOW

American Musical Theater Mural (Parts 3 and 4), 1999

TOP, LEFT TO RIGHT: George S. Kaufman, Sheldon Harnick, Philip Glass, Savion Glover, William Bolcom, Arnold Weinstein, Ntozake Shange, Laurie Anderson, and Anthony Davis.
BOTTOM, LEFT TO RIGHT: Mary Rodgers, Adam Guettel, Tom O'Horgan, Arthur Laurents, Jerry Bock, Charles Strouse, George C. Wolfe, Julie Taymor, Eliot Goldenthal, Thulani Davis, Lee Breuer, Ricky Ian Gordon, Garth Fagan, Meredith Monk, Jonathan Larson, Marjorie Samoff, and Alan Menken

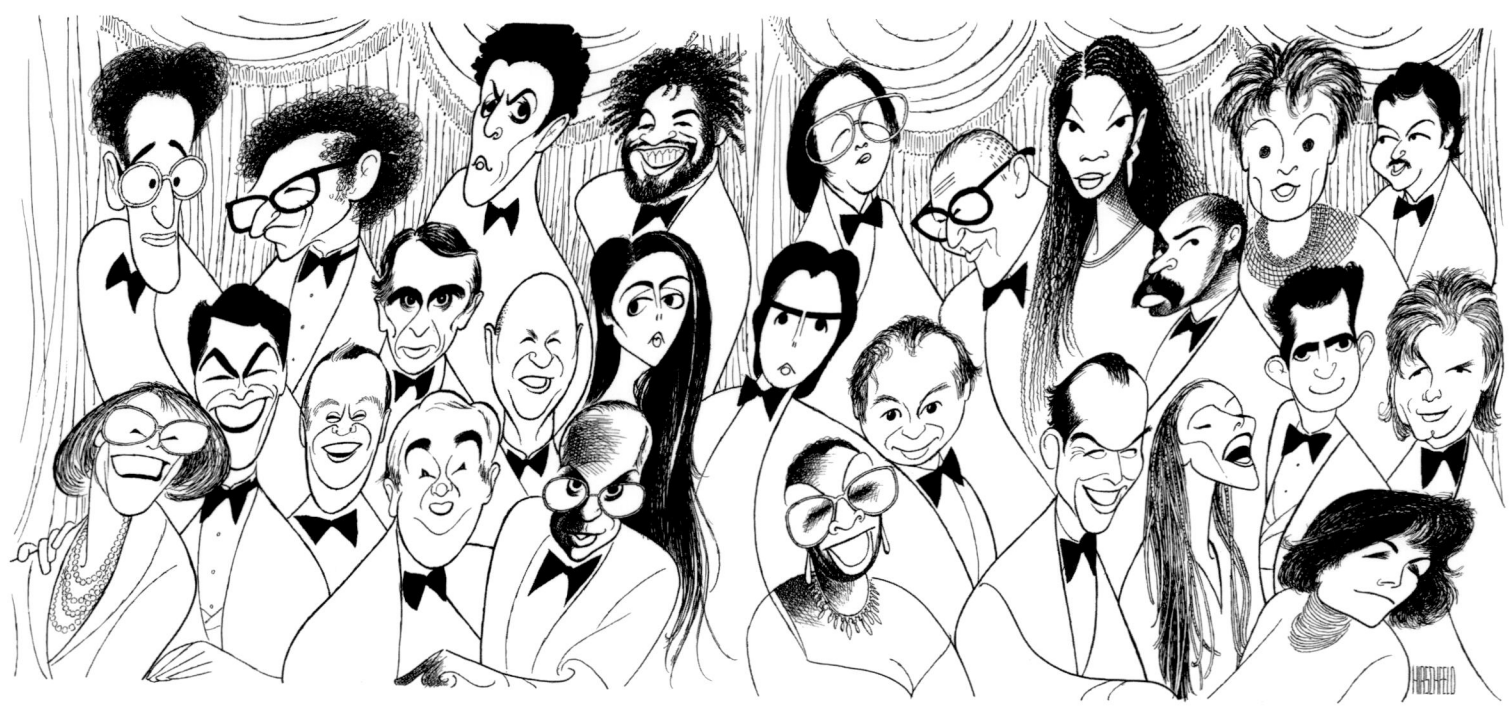

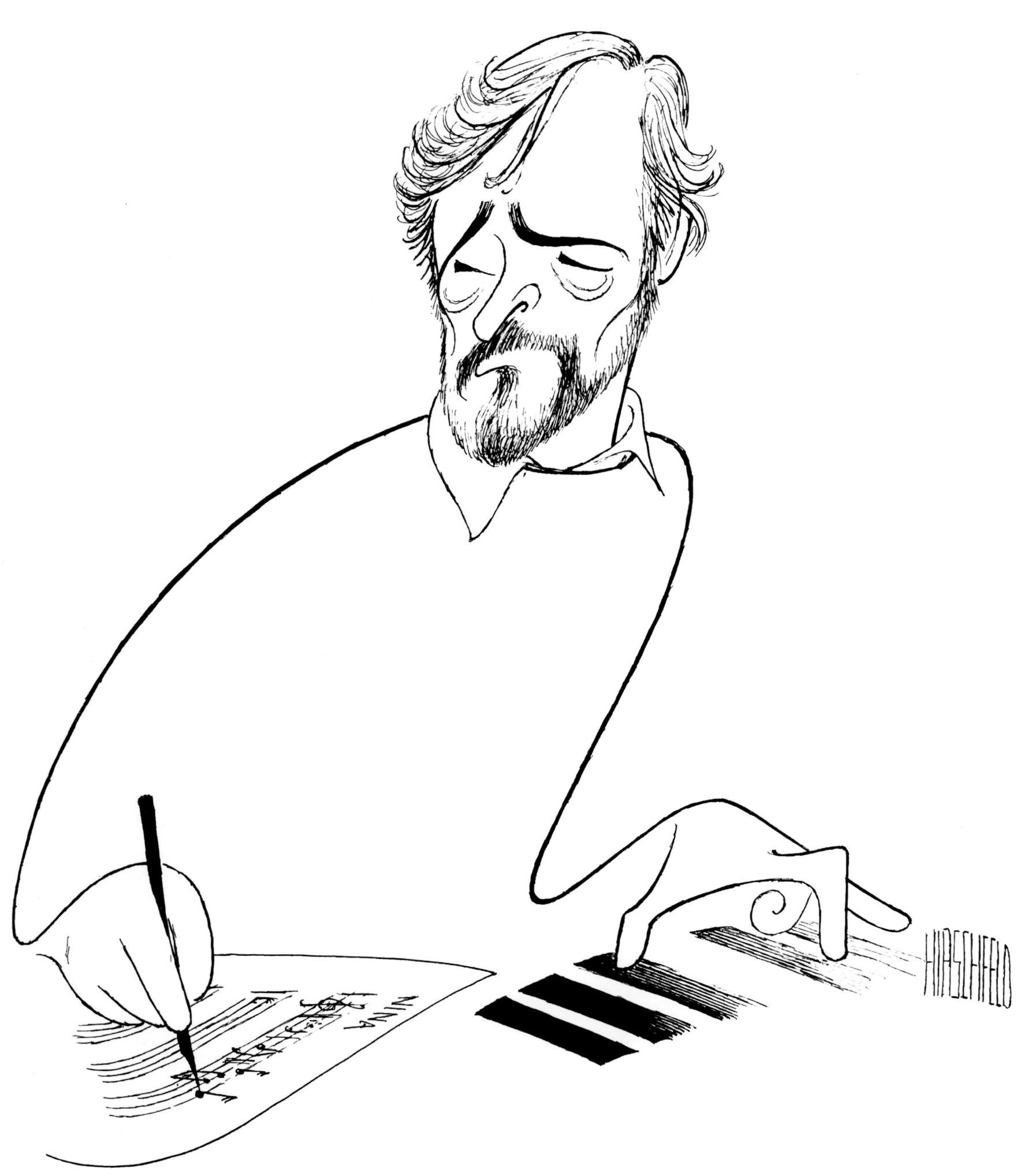

STEPHEN SONDHEIM

Ink on board, 1999

Unpublished

In 1977, in the *Times*' Friday theater column, there was a Hirschfeld portrait of Sondheim that is featured on the cover of this poster book. Typically, there were a few comments by the portrait subject in the column, but Sondheim refused to speak to the *Times*, so the column essentially ran gossip and publicly known information. This portrait of Sondheim has taken on a life of its own, becoming one of the most popular images of the composer.

Twenty-two years later, there was this private commission of a portrait of Sondheim. It showed the composer in a similar position at the piano while writing a song on staff paper. In both instances the song is about Hirschfeld's daughter, Nina. In the later portrait, the cigarette is gone (Sondheim gave up smoking in 1979 after a heart attack), but so are all the superfluous lines. His body is almost one long line, where Hirschfeld may have once felt obligated to delineate more. The hair is grayer, but the same intensity in his squint eye is still there. Hirschfeld and Sondheim agree: less is more.

Afterword
OFFSTAGE LINES

When Stephen Sondheim died, I quickly put together a Spotlight feature for our website, AlHirschfeldFoundation.org, that included every image of any show or film that Sondheim had written or contributed to. I was pleasantly surprised to see that there were more than fifty drawings covering almost the first half century of Sondheim—a remarkable overview of his career. The idea for this book was born that night.

It was not uncommon for Hirschfeld to capture someone's career in his art. Julie Harris, Carol Channing, Julie Andrews, Tennessee Williams, Laurel and Hardy, and many more fall into that category. Hirschfeld drew the world of entertainment for eighty-two years, starting at the age of seventeen when he created publicity drawings for the American release of *The Cabinet of Dr. Caligari* in 1920. His first caricature was published in 1925. He began to draw the theater in 1926. And his first drawing for the *New York Times* was in 1928. Although most of his contemporaries from the start of his career were at the end of theirs in 1957, when Hirschfeld drew *West Side Story*, he was not even halfway through his life's work.

I grew up in Harrisburg, Pennsylvania, where I had wonderful family and friends but nothing ever happened. Years later I would read a travel diary that S. J. Perelman kept of a trip he took around the world with Hirschfeld in 1947. In it he described a place as so boring it "was like rainy Sunday night in Rochester or any night in Harrisburg, Pennsylvania." I felt seen. Luckily, every Sunday morning a magic carpet—the Sunday *New York Times* Arts and Leisure section—arrived and took me to the mystical island of Manhattan, where all sorts of shows, concerts, dances, readings, and art were happening. When there was a Hirschfeld on the cover of the section, it only increased that sense of magic. I knew I had to get to the city one day.

While doing research on artist Ben Solowey in 1989, I saw that his "Theatre Portraits," charcoal drawings done from life of performers on Broadway and in opera and film, often ran side by side with Hirschfeld's in the *New York Times* and *Herald Tribune* from 1929 to 1942. I thought Hirschfeld might be able to provide more information on Solowey, so I looked him up in the phone book. I was too shy to call, so I wrote him a letter asking about Solowey, and two weeks later he sent back the warmest letter I have ever received from someone who was not a family member. He even invited me on my next visit to "Fun City" to come up and "quaff some tea."

I did, and we hit it off, but I soon learned that Hirschfeld hit it off with everyone. A short time later I was asked to organize his archive. As interesting as his life was, he had no interest in the past—he lived completely in the present. I was hired to think about his past, so when he was asked about it over the thirteen years we worked together, he would say things like "You'll have to talk to my archivist. He's put everything in order and now I can't find anything."

For me, Hirschfeld's studio was like King Tut's tomb—filled with unimaginable riches. Drawings, prints, magazines, clippings, books, a sign that read "Remember it was an actor who killed Lincoln," sculptures he had done as a teenager, and Balinese shadow puppets. He was always drawing. Someone always had an "assignment" for him. I worked right in his fourth-floor home studio, and when I found an item I needed more information on I would ask him, and he would answer while drawing. Occasionally he would stop—I think when I dislodged some long-forgotten memory—lean back in his chair, and tell an amusing little story, chuckle, then go back to drawing. He was resigned to getting the same ten questions from interviewers, but we frequently talked about drawings or stories that were comparatively obscure, although no less great than the ones most of his fans knew. At lunch, or over afternoon tea, we talked about art and theater, primarily what each of us had just seen or was going to see.

While he was alive, I wrote the book *Hirschfeld's Hollywood* for Abrams, which focused on his film art, and curated several museum exhibitions of his artwork, including the first comprehensive retrospective of his career. In 2015, my book *The Hirschfeld Century* was published to coincide with a major retrospective at the New York Historical Society. I am now the Creative Director of